MW01062059

I've known my friend and au~ And while I can say he has truly matured, he has not grown out of his passion for Jesus. It's tragic that some consider living without passion to be maturity. If anything, Todd's love for God is stronger now than in his early years. I'm also happy to be able to say that his love for Jesus can be measured by his love for people. He is continually moved with compassion for others. And I, for one, have been profoundly marked by his example in following Jesus with his whole heart. This wonderful book, *Life is Short—Leave a Legacy*, is his story of absolute surrender. This is a powerfully written testimony of the love of a good Father and His unending pursuit to see men and women set free for the honor of the name of Jesus. As you read this book, prepare your heart. Transformation and change are inevitable.

—BILL JOHNSON
BETHEL CHURCH
AUTHOR OF THE WAY OF LIFE AND HOPE IN ANY CRISIS

Todd White's life can best be described as a walking, breathing billboard for the vicarious atoning work of Christ. His passion for Jesus and reaching the lost stands second to none. This book is not a must read; it is a must do!

—SAMUEL RODRIGUEZ
NEW SEASON LEAD PASTOR, NHCLC PRESIDENT
AUTHOR OF YOU ARE NEXT
EXECUTIVE PRODUCER OF BREAKTHROUGH

If you've ever heard Todd White speak, you know he is passionate about his walk with the Lord. That same passion is evident on every page of this book as he shares the amazing testimony of how God led him from a life of drugs and immorality to a life of enthusiastic devotion to Him. I love to hear the stories of Todd's Spirit-led evangelism everywhere he goes, and I'm so glad to count him as a friend. I know you'll be encouraged as you read through this book.

–ROBERT MORRIS
GATEWAY CHURCH FOUNDING LEAD SENIOR PASTOR
BEST-SELLING AUTHOR OF THE BLESSED LIFE,
BEYOND BLESSED, AND TAKE THE DAY OFF

Todd White holds back nothing of his drama-filled life that went from deep darkness to a dazzling light in his love for Jesus. I'm honored to know him as my friend, as a man of God, both on and off stage, on continents and on islands in the Pacific. Millions have caught his contagious love for Jesus. You too will be impacted by his story, as I have been, when you read his book.

–LOREN CUNNINGHAM
YOUTH WITH A MISSION FOUNDER

It was an incredible honor for me to help publish Todd White's very first book and the first written account of the raw, full, detailed story of his amazing journey. Todd is a dear personal friend and is easily one of the most effective evangelists I've ever met. I have seen firsthand, behind the scenes, how he exudes passion for the lost. Evangelism is not an occupation to him—it is his lifestyle 24/7. His life is an example of obedience, hunger for God, and love for people. He is an inspiration to me and everyone who meets him. This book is packed full of the Word of God and firsthand examples of its power when put into action by a willing vessel. I believe, as you read through the pages of Todd's story, God is going to speak to you personally and help you to leave a legacy and to impact eternity for the glory of God.

–DANIEL KOLENDA
CHRIST FOR ALL NATIONS PRESIDENT AND CEO

LIFE IS SHORT—LEAVE A LEGACY

THE
TODD
WHITE
STORY

CfaN CHRIST FOR ALL NATIONS

Australia • Brazil • Canada • Czech Republic • Germany • Hong Kong • Kenya • Latin America
• Nigeria • New Zealand • Singapore • South Africa • United Kingdom • United States

Life Is Short—Leave a Legacy
Copyright © 2020 by Todd White

Published by Christ for all Nations
PO Box 590588
Orlando, FL 32859-0588, USA
Visit us online at: CfaN.org

ISBN 978-0-9894104-7-2

Editorial team—Sarah Thomas and Kimberly Overcast
Interior design—Deditorial Design
Cover design—Rafael Álvarez

All rights reserved. No part of this publication may be reproduced or transmitted in any form or by any means, electronic or mechanical, including photocopying, recording, or any information storage and retrieval system, without permission in writing from the author and publisher.

Unless otherwise noted, all Scripture quotations are taken from the New King James Version®. Copyright © 1982 by Thomas Nelson. Used by permission. All rights reserved.

Scripture quotations marked KJV are from the King James Version of the Bible.

Scripture quotations marked MEV are from the Modern English Version. Copyright © 2014 by Military Bible Association. Used by permission. All rights reserved.

Scripture quotations marked NIV are taken from the Holy Bible, New International Version®, NIV®. Copyright © 1973, 1978, 1984, 2011 by Biblica, Inc.® Used by permission of Zondervan. All rights reserved worldwide. www.zondervan.com. The "NIV" and "New International Version" are trademarks registered in the United States Patent and Trademark Office by Biblica, Inc.®

Scripture quotations marked NASB are from the New American Standard Bible, copyright © 1960, 1962, 1963, 1968, 1971, 1972, 1973, 1975, 1977, 1995 by The Lockman Foundation. Used by permission. www.Lockman.org

Printed in Colombia

I dedicate this book to anyone who feels lost, feels neglected, feels a lack of hope, feels a lack of destiny, or feels a lack of reason for being. I dedicate this book to all who are searching to find the answer to why they're alive. I dedicate this book to those trying to find their reason for being here. I dedicate this book to those who desire to find somebody to finally truly love them, to care about them, to be their everything. I dedicate this book to those who are searching to find the answer to the issues of life. I dedicate this book to those who are in despair, depressed, angry, bitter, ashamed, or afraid to go on. I dedicate this book to those who feel they've been abandoned.

But most of all I dedicate this book to my loving Father, who has changed everything through the blood of Jesus Christ.

Table of Contents

Acknowledgments

I'd like to acknowledge my dear wife, Jackie, and my beautiful children. Their patience, their trust, and their knowing that there's a call on my life as well as their lives allow me to be there when I can and gone when I need to be. Thank you so much for your grace, your love, and your understanding.

I'd like to acknowledge CfaN and Daniel Kolenda and the team for doing such an excellent job helping me write this book. It seemed an impossible endeavor, but Daniel has really shown me that it's possible. I'm excited to continue the journey of writing and pouring out my heart so that I can help someone somewhere understand that Jesus is King.

I also would like to thank Sarah Thomas, without your help this book would not have been written. You have the amazing ability to make a masterpiece out of what looked like a jumbled mess. Thank you so much for showing me what's possible. Great job!

I'd like to acknowledge all the men and women of God who have poured into my life over the years and have given me undoubtedly amazing treasures and absolutely outstanding revelation from their insights.

I acknowledge Dan Mohler for his dedication to seeing the best in me when I couldn't see anything. When my life was lost and I was blind and angry, Dan kept loving me and showing me what it was like to actually meet the Father. Thank you so much for your dedication and 100 percent obedience to the call of God on your life. It has made a substantial difference in my life and the lives of others affected by it.

Most of all, I acknowledge and give glory to my Father, who has done everything. God the Father, God the Son, and God the Holy Spirit, working together as one—thank You! Thank You! Thank You! I will enjoy eternity with You.

—Todd White

Chapter 1

Life Before Christ

One time when I shared my testimony with someone, he said, "That's an amazing story, man!" But I told him that it wasn't just a story; it was a testimony. The dictionary defines *testimony* as "firsthand authentication of a fact."[1] The Greek word for *testimony* in the Bible means "evidence given."[2] So a testimony is not just a story; it is an authentication, it is evidence, not only of what God has done but of what He wants to do again. So as you read my testimony in these pages, know that it is not meant to just be an entertaining read or a good story that blows your mind at times. It is evidence of what God can and will do for you, of what God wants to do for you. And know that *your* testimony of what God has done and is doing for you is just as powerful; the Word of God says so:

They overcame him by the blood of the Lamb and by the word of their testimony.

—Revelation 12:11

My testimony begins with darkness, which entered my life at an early age. I discovered pornography and masturbation when I was only eight years old and quickly became consumed by it. My parents did not belong to Christ at that time, and they were having marriage problems. I need to tell you that they are now saved, Spirit-filled, and fully serving the Lord with their lives today! They are amazing people with incredible testimonies. However, while I was growing up, they were deeply hurting, and because of the hurt, their relationship with each other was suffering. This was decades before they were saved; they didn't know any better because they had no relationship with Jesus. They began growing further apart, and eventually the entire marriage collapsed.

My mom told my dad to leave when I was eleven and a half years old, and it completely broke me. My two younger sisters were too little to understand, but I knew what was happening, and I totally derailed. For the first time, rage and hate entered my heart. I became an uncontrollable, bitter, angry kid, who wouldn't listen to anyone. The Bible calls this type of anger the root of bitterness that defiles many.

Pursue peace with all people, and holiness, without which no one will see the Lord: looking carefully lest anyone fall short of the grace of God; lest any root of bitterness springing up cause trouble, and by this many become defiled.

—Hebrews 12:14–15

I began getting into fights at school, and I bullied people around so much that oftentimes I had to eat lunch in the principal's office, separate from the other students. My anger was unmanageable, as I didn't know how to deal with the absence of my father. I screamed and cussed at my mother, destroyed things, and caused all kinds of chaos. My wild behavior escalated so much that she couldn't handle me and didn't know where to turn for help. During this time, one of her jobs was working at a pizza restaurant, and her boss happened to be a thirty-second degree Mason. He told her there was a place I could go where I would be taken care of and get the help I needed. It was a boys' home sponsored by the Freemasons. They provided everything for the kids there, meaning she wouldn't have to pay a penny. As a single mom working three jobs, this seemed like the only good option for her situation.

When we went to visit the Masonic Homes, I noticed they had playgrounds, softball fields, and a huge gymnasium. To me, the place looked like the ideal escape plan. At first my mom told me I would come home at the end of the summer. But after summer ended, she said that due to finances and the pressure she was under, she wasn't ready for me to come home yet. The truth was that she was very afraid the mayhem I had caused before would all return if I went home. I ended up staying at the Masonic Homes for five and a half years. Periodically I went to see my dad and spend time with him, but when it was time to visit my mom, I immediately went to my friend's house. I still held great resentment against my mom for kicking my dad out. My friend and I spent our time smoking weed, and I loved it. You see, when I was high, all of my problems and pain went away. It was a false sense of peace, coming from a drug that made me feel like I was OK—but I was definitely not OK!

By the time I was twelve years old, I was fully addicted to drugs. I was taking acid and mushrooms, drinking as much alcohol as I could get away with, and smoking weed every day. I would have injected drugs into my veins as well if I hadn't been so afraid of needles. Thankfully I steered clear of those. There were no Christian influences anywhere around me, and I never heard the gospel. There was no one speaking into my life or pouring God's love into me. I was absolutely miserable! Drugs and pornography were my sources of comfort, but they weren't enough. I pressed further into darkness with Ouija boards, séances, and dark music and fantasies. I began to live more in fantasies than I lived in reality.

While I was in the boys' home, I took a martial arts class to learn how to defend myself from getting beat up by the other kids. I was a fighter and an aggressor. I continued to spiral downward into addiction, depression, and self-hatred as time went on. You see, I was still grieving the absence of my father and the life we had before my family was radically torn apart. After five and a half years at the boys' home, my roommate and best friend in the home, Larry, had a complete meltdown and began acting out in a crazy manner. As a result he was kicked out of the boys' home, and I found my next escape plan. I thought I would try the same thing to get kicked out, and sure enough, it worked. My dad came to get me and took me to my mom's house. My mom had remarried, and now I had a stepdad whom I really didn't want in my life. He tried to be a father to me, but I wasn't having it. I did everything I could to cause problems between him and my mom. Finally my stepdad gave my mom an ultimatum. She had to choose: it was either him or me. One of us had to go. When I got into fights with my mom and stepdad, I would leave and go to a friend's house. I floated around from one friend's house to another, just to stay away from my mom and stepdad.

During high school, I signed up to join the navy. It seemed like another great escape plan at the time. However, six months before graduation, I realized that wasn't the kind of escape I wanted. The drugs were working like a charm, and the navy didn't sound appealing to me anymore. But there was a small problem. The only way to get out of the document I signed to join the navy was to not graduate from high school. Realizing my predicament, I began to fail all of my classes on purpose so that my navy program could be canceled.

Right after high school was over and I was out of the navy contract, I took summer classes to get my diploma. I was trying to get my act together because I wanted to do something good with my life. Then my stepdad said, "You can never be a real man because real men are marines." I thought, "I'll show you!" So I joined the marines. I went to boot camp with an attitude problem. I was mouthing off the whole time. Now, as you can imagine, when you're in boot camp, it's not a good idea to mouth off. I told them what I thought, and they showed me what they thought! For thirteen weeks they tried to break me. I was the king of the quarterdeck! That means I received extra attention in physical training. The goal was to whip me into submission and conformity. Seventy-two pounds later, I was a machine!

When I graduated from boot camp, my mom and stepdad came down to see me. With tears streaming down her face, Mom said, "You've changed."

I said, "Yes ma'am." But it didn't last long...only twelve days, to be exact.

I went home for a couple of weeks, then returned to the base. When I got back to the base, I learned that these marines were party machines! So I went out with them and had fun, drinking and getting high. The next thing you know, I was consumed. My life was right back where it had been before. You see, brainwashing isn't the way to go. Blood washing is the only way! My heart needed to be cleansed by the blood of Jesus, and my brain needed to be washed by the blood of Jesus. It's the blood of Jesus that cleanses your conscience.

> Not with the blood of goats and calves, but with His own blood He entered the Most Holy Place once for all, having obtained eternal redemption.
>
> —HEBREWS 9:12

But I didn't understand any of this yet. I couldn't handle being a marine and decided to go home...illegally. I went

AWOL, which in the marines is called UA, or unauthorized absence. My mom was surprised to see that I was home, so I lied and told her I was on leave. While I was out, I stole a large amount of money in a drug deal and then ran out to Colorado with four of my friends. I told them I would pay their way to come with me with the money I had stolen. We stayed in Colorado for about six months, living in hotels and partying.

One day we were driving to another city with open beers in the truck. All of my buddies were underage, so I knew we were in trouble when a police officer pulled us over. I told my friends that once the cop found out who I was, I would be arrested and taken into custody. The officer took my driver's license back to his car to look me up. Within minutes several squad cars pulled up. Five officers got out, surrounded my truck, and pointed their 9mm guns at me. That was it. I knew our joyride was officially over. They took me to the county jail and called the military. The military sent two bounty hunters to get me and take me to the military prison. They put me in an orange jumpsuit, shackled me up in chains, and extradited me back across America. I was in the brig for five and a half months.

Because of my attitude problem I was often segregated and put in solitary confinement. After I was released, they sent me to a base in North Carolina to await orders for discharge. They told me it would take a year and a half to clear my orders. I couldn't wait that long, so within two months I ran away again. I loved to ski, so I flew back to Colorado. That wasn't very smart since it would make me easier to find. I reunited with all of my friends, who now had jobs. I was able to get a job working at a really nice ski resort. My new employer didn't investigate my background, and they gave me the keys to over one hundred properties, worth more than a million dollars each. My job was to shovel snow in the driveways, then go inside to check on the pipes. But of course I had other plans! After I shoveled snow at these beautiful homes, I went inside and sat around, watched their TVs, and smoked weed. I did nothing except goof off until three o'clock when I got off work. Then I would go skiing. Every day I woke up and did the routine all over again. My life was one long party. I acted like a ski bum, but I was really a skiing fugitive. I made it almost an entire year before I was found and arrested again.

One day I was sitting in the hot tub at the resort's clubhouse with my friends. We had been smoking weed, and we were completely stoned. A police officer walked in and asked if any of us knew Todd White. We played dumb and said no. The cop lied and told us they were trying to get in touch with Todd because one of his family members was really ill. I was high and feeling paranoid and worried, so I tried calling my mom to find out what was going on. She didn't answer, so then I called the police station, claiming to be a friend who would be able to "give Todd a message" for them. The lady on the phone put me on hold.

While I was still on the phone, the same police officer came in, showed me my picture, and said, "Why did you lie to me?"

I said, "Why do you think?"

I was arrested and taken to jail. The military sent the bounty hunters again. They extradited me back across America, and I went back to the brig for six more months. Being in prison didn't change anything. I still had the same attitude problem, the same rebellious behavior toward authority. I hadn't learned anything from my mistakes. Sin isn't something you can educate yourself out of. Only Jesus can set you free!

The military then gave me what is known as a big chicken dinner, or bad conduct discharge (BCD). At this point, my life was a total train wreck! Having a BCD on your record doesn't look very good, so the only job I could land was in sales. It was commission based. I could work anywhere, and the money I made was equal to whatever I could sell. I became a con artist, a manipulator, and a liar. I could manipulate anyone to get my way. I was as selfish as selfish can be.

It would be a very sad fact if we were in the kingdom and were selfish still. That's why Jesus said to deny yourself, pick up your cross, and "follow Me."

When He had called the people to Himself, with His disciples also, He said to them, "Whoever desires to come after Me, let him deny himself, and take up his cross, and follow Me."

—Mark 8:34

Righteousness is the opposite of selfishness—the complete opposite! You see, when I am right with God, and I see the reality of who God says I am, all of a sudden my life enters this place where righteousness keeps me.

But seek first the kingdom of God and His righteousness, and all these things shall be added to you.

—MATTHEW 6:33

The Bible doesn't say to seek things; it says to seek Him. So, as I seek God and spend time with Him, I see Him, and I become like Him. And as I think in my heart, so I am.

For the kingdom of God is not eating and drinking, but righteousness and peace and joy in the Holy Spirit.

—ROMANS 14:17

For as he thinks in his heart, so is he. "Eat and drink!" he says to you, but his heart is not with you.

—PROVERBS 23:7

So the kingdom of God is in the Holy Spirit, and the first thing the Holy Spirit reveals is the reality of my right standing with God. Then peace with God comes from having right standing with Him. And when I have peace with God, then I can actually walk in the joy of my salvation. This is totally amazing and beautiful. If God can touch me, He can touch anybody!

I floated around from one commission job to another, and I was really good at sales. I was a habitual liar, and I would tell anyone what they wanted to hear in order to get my way. I had sold drugs since I was little, so I used that same skill to sell products. It didn't matter if I believed in the product or not—I could sell it. Finally I landed a job working for a guy who was selling alarm systems. I went into people's homes and scared them with stories about break-ins and burglaries. Little did they know that some of my knowledge was based on my personal experience breaking and entering homes and stealing from people. I conjured up really scary stories and raised the fear factor in hopes that potential buyers would want to purchase an alarm system from me. The manipulation was working, and I sold a bunch of security systems by selling fear to people.

My boss knew nothing of my drug abuse and history of poor behavior. He genuinely thought I was a good guy—a top salesman who just drank a little on the side. He told me his wife knew this wonderful girl named Jackie, and he wanted to introduce me to her. He set us up on a blind date. I ended up schmoozing her and tricking her into thinking I was a great guy—some sort of stallion—because I was a great liar, just like the father of lies. That is why it's so dangerous for Christians to lie. The problem is they don't want to tell great big lies; they just want to call them little white lies. Hey, a little white lie is the same as a great big lie! A lie is a lie, no matter how small it is. It's the same thing! The Bible says that Satan is the father of lies.

> You are of your father the devil, and you want to do the desires of your father. He was a murderer from the beginning, and does not stand in the truth because there is no truth in him. Whenever he speaks a lie, he speaks from his own nature, for he is a liar and the father of lies.
>
> —JOHN 8:44, NASB

God forbid that you manipulate the truth just a little bit, let your kids see it, and then try to get them to be on fire for Jesus. The number one thing Jesus rebuked was hypocrisy.

> You blind guides! You strain out a gnat but swallow a camel. Woe to you, teachers of the law and Pharisees, you hypocrites! You clean the outside of the cup and dish, but inside they are full of greed and self-indulgence.
>
> —MATTHEW 23:24–25, NIV

So I went on a blind date with this amazing girl and convinced her I was an amazing guy. I was such a con artist. You see, Jackie had been married once before. Her ex-husband was emotionally and verbally abusive. She had already been through so much with him, including two full-term stillborn babies due to an extremely rare complication called prune belly syndrome. After it happened the second time, Jackie was told she could never have a child that would survive the pregnancy. To add insult to injury, her marriage soon unraveled, leaving her divorced and completely brokenhearted. So, when she met me a year later, she thought her worst days were over. I seemed like a knight in shining armor. We fell in love and moved in together.

At that point, Jackie knew nothing of my drug use and wanted to have a child with me. Despite the dismal prognosis she'd been given, we began infertility treatments in hopes of having a viable pregnancy. About a year later we found out we were pregnant with a baby girl and decided that if she survived, we would name her Destiny—if she made it, that name would be perfect! Months later our beautiful Destiny was born healthy and thriving! It was a happy moment and then a sad moment, all at the same time. It quickly became apparent to everyone that I was not the stand-up guy I had made myself out to be. In fact I wasn't standing up at all!

The day Destiny arrived I was so high and drunk I could barely walk, and I wound up passed out, facedown on the hospital floor! I literally wasn't in a position to be a doting husband and father. I wasn't even sober enough to hold my baby girl. The cracks in my facade were beginning to show. All of a sudden I found myself looking at this baby, and I realized I was a total failure and a drug addict. At that point I was not a believer, and Christianity wasn't even on my grid. There I was, looking at my daughter, thinking, "I'm a failure—I'm done. I cannot do this!" You see, I had always been able to come up with an escape plan, but the one thing I could never seem to escape was myself.

Fear and despair gripped my heart, and I began to have suicidal thoughts on a regular basis. My mind was constantly bombarded with imaginations of ways I could kill myself. I was extremely depressed and hearing voices. All I could think about was ending my life. Now, what was happening to me was very demonic, but I didn't understand that. I went to see doctors to get antidepressants to help me calm down. The demonic influence I was under was ferocious, and no matter how many drugs I took or how much weed I smoked, it wasn't enough! I kept taking more and more drugs just to take the edge off, just to cope with everything that was going on in my head. The reality of my life was upon me, and I couldn't handle it. I knew I was supposed to step up to the proverbial plate, but I couldn't do it.

Some people say, "When I had my kids, everything changed for the better." Well, that's not how it was for me when I had my daughter. Everything just got worse! I realized I couldn't be a dad because I was so messed up. I was in constant turmoil. I would wake up in the morning and do bong hits to get high. When I would start to come down, I'd have another "one-hitter" at work to pick me back up, and then I'd get drunk and high again at night. It was all day, every day, and I could no longer hide my addictions from my girlfriend. Jackie was getting fed up with me. I couldn't hold a job. I would get hired and then terminated soon after because I was caught stealing, because I was high on drugs, or because I simply didn't show up to work. My life was severely self-destructive. Jackie watched me go through three different jobs and realized we were never going to get out of the run-down trailer we were living in or provide anything nice for our daughter.

One day Jackie said, "I am leaving you! I hate you!" Like me, she was an atheist, had no Christians in her family, and had no godly influence in her life.

When she told me she was done, I said, "If you leave me, I'll kill myself and leave our daughter without a father." Jackie knew it wasn't just crazy talk—the threat was real. She was afraid of what I would do to myself, because it wasn't just during daytime hours that I was being tormented by thoughts of death. I was consistently waking up in the middle of the night, having nightmares about killing myself. I thought about ways to end my life around the clock, and she knew it. She reluctantly stayed and walked on pins and needles around me, trying not to set me off and constantly worried about what I might do to myself if she were to leave.

Looking back at the man I was and the things I said and did, it's as if I am talking about a completely different man. I remember saying and doing those things, but the man I used to be is so far removed from the man I am today. Praise Jesus! I'm a new creation in Christ today! I'm free today! I'm clean today! The problem was I had an unclean spirit back then. Those voices telling me to end my life were demonic spirits from hell sent to torment me and stop the plan of God from being fulfilled in my life.

The Bible talks about a man Jesus met right after He stepped foot in the country of the Gadarenes. The man had an unclean spirit. He lived among the tombs, and he couldn't be tamed. He would cut himself with sharp stones and cry aloud day and night in agony. (See Mark 5:1–20 and Luke 8:26–39.) You see, suicidal thoughts are from the kingdom of darkness and death. It's no wonder this poor man dwelt among the tombs and spent his days compulsively causing himself harm—that's exactly what the devil has planned for all of humanity. Jesus called Satan a thief that has come to kill, steal, and destroy.

> The thief does not come except to steal, and to kill, and to destroy. I have come that they may have life, and that they may have it more abundantly.
>
> —John 10:10

What a stark contrast between the plan of Satan for your life and the plan of God for your life! Jesus had a plan for the man from the tombs that was completely opposite from the painful life of bondage and sorrow he was accustomed to. The moment Jesus set him free, his life was set on a whole new trajectory into a victorious existence full of peace, freedom, and an abundance of joy! This same man, once bound and tormented by a legion of monstrous spirits, went on to proclaim the good news of the Savior to an entire region of desperate people who marveled at what the Lord had done. They were filled with hope beyond what they ever knew was possible! This is the power of God—and it makes all the difference.

But after my daughter was born, I had no knowledge of how captive I was, much less the power of God to deliver me. I was still among the tombs, and just like the straw that broke the camel's back, it would only be a matter of time before the pressure would make me snap.

Chapter 2

Hopeless View of Life

Life without Christ is truly a hopeless existence. However, when I saw Christians out in the world, I didn't witness anything different that gave me any kind of hope for something better. The Christians I saw in restaurants after church on Sunday were all dressed up on the outside, but they were obviously mean on the inside. They were the biggest complainers! They were nasty to their servers and acted horribly to their family members. If they were like this in public, what were they like behind closed doors? I remember thinking, "What is wrong with these people?"

Sometimes I watched Christian television while I was sitting at home getting high. It looked like a production—some sort of act to create an emotional experience that would inspire people to send them money. I saw people with their hands raised and pastor's wives talking and crying with tons of mascara running down their faces, and I wondered why they were doing all of this. I flipped through the Christian television channels and listened to these people preach, and to me it seemed as if they were putting on a show. Nothing about it felt real. Plus I never saw Christians practice what they preached. Christianity just seemed like an emotional crutch for people who couldn't handle their lives. The Christians I met at work were way more worried than everyone else. They would easily crumble apart when life got tough. I remember making fun of them because they would make all of these big claims about their faith, but their lives didn't back it up—there was no lasting good fruit that came from it. In fact, if anything, there was evidence of bad fruit!

Now, you must understand that I was a fault finder. I was looking for bad things so I could mock these people and discredit their entire message. I intentionally looked for ways to debate with Christians and pick them apart. I must say, they were easy targets. You see, my negative opinion of believers was not just based on the ones I met through work or observed at restaurants. I also remember hearing the news of multiple scandals involving high-profile ministers being caught in everything from affairs to embezzlement, even being thrown into prison for breaking the law. These were supposedly people of God! These were ministers who paraded themselves on TV as holy examples of Jesus on the earth, but instead of displaying Jesus, they displayed really bad conduct. To me, Christianity was a joke! It was repulsive. The only benefit

I found to Christianity was that it was fun to mock, and it gave me an advantage in product sales—meaning I had heard just enough of the typical Christian vocabulary to act like one when I needed to sell products to Christians. If I walked in a home and saw a cross up on the wall, I would use my "Christian card" and play the part to help make the sale. What I didn't understand back then is that what I had observed my whole life was not true Christianity. I had been witnessing a people in a religion *about* Jesus instead of a people in a relationship *with* Jesus.

As I mentioned before, I had played with Ouija boards and participated in séances. I had also gone to mediums, so I wasn't closed off to the supernatural world. In fact I found the spirit world to be a thrilling adventure! I had seen some powerful things—dark things, but they were real. Christianity wasn't thrilling to me. I thought Christians were boring stuffed shirts who acted a certain way in the church and a completely different way outside of it. People are intrinsically hungry for the supernatural because we are spirit beings—but unfortunately many churches have a form of godliness but deny its power!

> But know this, that in the last days perilous times will come: For men will be . . . having a form of godliness but denying its power. And from such people turn away!
>
> —2 Timothy 3:1-2, 5

I pressed into as much of the supernatural realm as I could because I was spiritually hungry. Many people are seeking out the supernatural world. You see this happening with the rise in television shows and movies about mediums talking to the dead, aliens and extraterrestrial beings, vampires, werewolves, angels, zombies, and witches. It's important to note that darkness has a limited amount of power; Christianity has an endless source of power, but so few of us ever tap into it. What would happen if *all* Christians started tapping into the power available to each and every believer?

> Most assuredly, I say to you, he who believes in Me, the works that I do he will do also; and greater works than these he will do, because I go to My Father.
>
> —JOHN 14:12

The world is pressing deeper into magic, but magic is just an illusion. Jesus is the complete opposite of illusion. He is the truth. He is healing, miracles, signs, and wonders. He didn't just levitate—He walked on water, walked through walls, and ascended into heaven with hundreds of people watching.

> Jesus said to him, "I am the way, the truth, and the life. No one comes to the Father except through Me."
>
> —JOHN 14:6

When I was pursuing the dark world of magic, I was pursuing something that had such small power, not knowing there was One who had such great power, and He was waiting for me in the light.

So Jackie continued to be terrified that I might harm myself or end up dead in a ditch somewhere—she knew I had made enemies out of all the people I had ripped off. I had stolen so much money from people. I had even stolen drugs from drug dealers, which is a super dangerous thing to do. She stayed for seven and a half years of my acting like this, mostly out of fear of what I might do to myself or what might be done to me if I were left all alone. During those seven and a half years, she held the same job she had when we first got together, while I bounced around from one job to the next. I went through a total of thirty different jobs in the same time frame. Every time I got a new job, I would either quit or get fired shortly after getting the job. And I stole from everybody.

When I was in sales, I would go to job sites at people's homes, and I would ask to use their restrooms so I could go through their medicine cabinets to pick out whatever pills I thought would help me. I was a totally twisted drug addict, hooked on cocaine, and I was becoming an expert thief. I was also known as the black sheep of the family. When I came around, family members hid their purses and wallets. I was a really mean guy with a very bad attitude and explosive behavior. On more than one occasion, when someone behind me at a stoplight honked at me, I got out of my car, went to the car behind me, got the person who honked to open his window, and then punched him. I was a very bad man—and that's not the half of it! I was completely tormented by my own existence.

Finally my girlfriend couldn't handle me anymore. I came home one night to find that she had left with my seven-and-a-half-year-old daughter. They were gone. I was done! I knew she wasn't with anybody, but I was at the end of my rope. I didn't want to live anymore, so I decided to make good on my threat and end my life. I went to Jackie's stepdad's house to get a rifle because he owned a bunch of guns. While I was there, I saw a phone book next to the pen and pad I was going to use to leave a suicide note. For some reason I grabbed the phone book and opened it. It opened to a list of churches. There were 586 churches listed there (I know because I counted them later). I didn't know who to call. I grabbed a marker, drew a circle around one of those churches, and decided to go there. I didn't even know why I was going, but God knew. He was drawing me, but I had no clue. I was totally oblivious to it all.

No one can come to Me unless the Father who sent Me draws him; and I will raise him up at the last day.

–JOHN 6:44

When I got to the church, a man with the biggest smile on his face met me at the door. He said, "How are you doing, buddy?"

I couldn't figure out why he was so happy and smiling, so I said, "I'm not your buddy." I wondered what was wrong with the man. Such happiness didn't make sense to me. I went inside and began telling him all of my problems. The head pastor of the church wasn't there. The guy I was talking with was Dan Mohler, the associate pastor of the church at that time. Dan began to talk to me about Jesus. I said, "Man, I didn't come here to hear about Jesus!"

He said, "This is a church."

So I said, "Why are you so happy, man? What's wrong with you?" (Still, to this day, you can't get the smile off of

Dan's face. It's crazy!) I've come to discover that as a man thinks in his heart, so is he. That's why Dan is so happy!

For as he thinks in his heart, so is he.

—Proverbs 23:7

So I went back to pouring out all of my problems. He said, "You've got to hear what Jesus did! Let me tell you what Jesus did for you!" But I was aggravated, and I told him that he wasn't listening to me. He said, "I am listening, but what you're telling me isn't helping you. You told me that you came here because you were going to end your life. So why don't you give your life to somebody who wants it?"

"Why would anyone want my life, knowing all the things I've done and all the stuff I've been into?"

"That's just it—it's not about what you've done. It's about what Jesus has done *for you!*"

"How could some dead guy want my life?"

"He's not dead. He's alive!"

Then he began to share the gospel with me again. It was the first time I had ever heard a Christian share the gospel. In fact it was the first time I had ever heard the gospel, period! Dan didn't say, "You need to invite Jesus into your heart." He told me to give Jesus my life. It would be bad if I invited Jesus into my heart but held back my life.

I knew my life was falling apart, so I said, "OK. Whatever, man. Fine!" That was my first acceptance of Jesus: "Fine! Whatever! I don't want my life anyway!" I had no idea what I was getting into—not a clue! But something had brought me to that church. There was something in me that believed what Dan had told me. You see, the more Dan shared the gospel with me, the more the truth became real to me. Dan was the first authentic Christian I had ever met. I told him, "If God is real, then He is going to be really happy with you!" I could barely stand to look in his eyes. I could see the light of God in him. He was the real deal, and I could see the Lord in him by just looking in his eyes!

> The eye is the lamp of the body; so then if your eye is clear, your whole body will be full of light.
>
> —MATTHEW 6:22, NASB

I was looking at a man who was filled with light, the Word of God, and pure love! I desperately wanted what he had and what he was talking about, but in my mind I thought I was too far away from being there. I didn't understand that it started from a confession of faith, because I had previously understood Christianity to be about works. I thought reaching God was like climbing a ladder of good works—one good work on top of another. I had such a deficit in good works and such a copious amount of bad works, it seemed downright impossible for me to become anything like what I was seeing in Dan. But that kind of thinking was all wrong! That is what religion does. It's nothing close to what Jesus does! Religion compares people; Jesus captivates people! I still didn't understand that, so I became agitated and told Dan I had to leave. Dan gave me his number so that I could keep in touch. I resisted at first but finally took it on my way out. From that day forward my life was never the same. A seed had been planted in my heart.

I went home and called Jackie to tell her she needed to come home. Destiny answered the phone. Jackie didn't want to talk to me. I said, "Tell Mommy she needs to come home."

She said, "Daddy, Mommy isn't coming home. She said she hates you."

I said, "You need to tell Mommy that Daddy found God."

My daughter paused and said, "What's He like, Dad?"

I said, "I don't know, but I met somebody who does. I went to see a man at church who told me his God is going to change my life." Reluctantly Jackie returned home with my daughter.

Chapter 3

Jesus Incorporated

The night my girls returned home, I went to put my daughter to bed, and she told me how happy she was that I had found God and that I was going to get better. I told her how much I loved her and promised I would never put her and her mother through this again. I cried, held her close, and kissed her good night. Then I made my way to the couch because Jackie wouldn't allow me to sleep in the bed with her. In fact most nights the couch was my doghouse. An hour later I broke out my bong and some beers and started to get high. About six beers later I was overcome with an uncontrollable urge for crack cocaine. Hell-bent with a one-track mind, I went out on another binge. The first night they were back–imagine that.

At 4:30 the next morning I walked back in the house. Jackie and Destiny were up waiting for me on the sofa. Jackie was wide awake and infuriated. Every day she told my daughter that she hated me and was going to leave me as soon as Destiny was old enough. She told her that I only cared about myself. See, even though Jackie wasn't saved, she was responsible. She was the one making money for our family, and I was the one who had put us through debt, bankruptcy, repossessions, and warrants out for my arrest for not paying my bills. Jackie wasn't perfect, but she couldn't see any of her own faults or failures because she was so focused on mine.

As soon as I walked in the house that morning, she began screaming at me. She told me she hated me and called me a hypocrite. I became very angry, especially because I couldn't stand being called that word—hypocrite. That's what I had always accused Christians of being! It is what I hated the most about Christians, and it only took one night for me to earn that title.

I called Dan that morning and shouted, "Your Jesus doesn't work! Nothing has changed! Look, I went out and used cocaine again—I didn't want to do it, but I did it again!"

He said, "Todd, how do you feel?"

"I feel horrible!" I screamed.

"Todd, do you realize that just a couple days ago you didn't feel anything like this? Right now you feel horrible after doing this, but just a couple days ago you wouldn't have felt anything like you feel now, which shows me that there's a seed growing in your heart!"

"Well, make it grow faster!" I shouted. I threw the phone down and stormed off to my basement to get high and escape all that I was feeling.

Meanwhile my girlfriend was upstairs stomping around, seething mad, functioning on little sleep, trying to get ready for work, and trying to get my daughter ready for school. It was awful!

For the next five and a half months, I did everything possible to damage myself and my family with my addictions. Four or five times a week I was out doing drugs. I called Dan every morning and told him, "Man, I did it again!"

He responded by telling me what the Bible says about who I am in Christ. He quoted scripture after scripture, but he never clobbered me over the head with it; he gently spoon-fed it into my heart. Day after day I failed again and then called Dan yet again. You know what he never told me? He never told me that I had a chemical imbalance or that my serotonin levels were off or that all I needed to do was follow a twelve-step program in order to keep myself on the right track. You see, I had tried all of those methods before, but they didn't last. Dan was different. He believed in a one-step program: submission to God.

When people submit to the Lord, they are submitting themselves to Him entirely and simultaneously resisting the devil! Submission to God means submitting to the truth—which is His Word—making it more valuable than anything. It also means submitting yourself to His Holy Spirit, allowing the blood of Jesus to do the proper cleansing of your life. His blood cleanses you from all sin, and you become a brand-new creation! Old things pass away, and all things become new! You actually become a new creation!

> Therefore submit to God. Resist the devil and he will flee from you.
>
> —JAMES 4:7

> Therefore, if anyone is in Christ, he is a new creation; old things have passed away; behold, all things have become new.
>
> —2 CORINTHIANS 5:17

At this point in my life my friends and I had been in a heavy rock band for about three years. We held band practice in the basement of my home. We had a very talented group of guys, and we took our music seriously. The songs I wrote were about anger, rage, beating people up, sex, lust, and all kinds of twisted topics that get people rowdy. Once I found Jesus, I didn't feel right singing those kinds of songs anymore. I told the guys all about meeting with Dan and giving my life to God, because I wanted them to believe in Him too. But they attacked me with obscenities and repeatedly told me to shut up. I was still doing drugs, and there was nothing significantly different about my life other than my proclamation that Jesus is real. They didn't want to hear about it. I had no idea what I was doing. On one hand I wanted to take drugs and party, but on the other hand I wanted to talk about Dan's God. I knew what I saw in Dan was real, and I just couldn't keep it to myself! Then I started incorporating

Jesus into the songs we were singing. Three of the band members became so irate with me that they stormed out with all of their equipment.

There was one guy who didn't leave—Bobby. Bobby was my best friend. When he was just thirteen years old, he was riding his bike down a hill when he hit a chain link fence the state had put up to barricade the park. He hit the fence so hard in such a way that it tore him open right through the middle. He was literally gutted to the point that his intestines came out. He would have died, but someone found him on the road and rushed him to the hospital. They put him back together, and he healed over time. However, due to the cause of the incident, Bobby received a huge settlement from the state when he turned eighteen. Later on he met a girl, fell in love, and got married. They had two children, and he became a stay-at-home dad.

Thanks to the settlement from the state, money was not an issue for Bobby, so he spent his days doing what he loved. He became an amazing self-taught guitarist, and his schedule was so free that he was usually available to talk, hang out, and practice with me. We spent a lot of time together, meeting at least twice a week. I confided in him about things I would never tell anyone else. Bobby wasn't into cocaine, but he loved his cannabis. We smoked *a lot* of weed when we were together. He drove an hour and a half to my house to practice with me in my basement. Sometimes I would be out late on a crack binge, and he would drive all the way to my house for our scheduled practice time, just to end up practicing all by himself in my basement while I was out doing drugs.

Bobby didn't believe in Jesus, but he was my best friend. I tried to get him to meet with me and Dan multiple times, but he wouldn't do it. He was a chilled-out, passive kind of guy, and he told me he was glad I had found my path, but that's as far as he wanted to go with the subject. He said things such as, "I don't believe in Jesus, man, but I believe in you. OK, bro? You are what you make yourself, man, and I know you've got problems, but I'm here for you."

Bobby tried to get me to go to rehab. He knew I was hooked on crack, and he could tell I was spiraling out of control. He really cared about me and wanted me to get some help. Even though our band had broken up, Bobby and I continued to meet together on our own. Soon after that I was upstairs raging mad at my girlfriend and my daughter, yelling and screaming, and I punched a hole in the door. Then I went down to the basement to greet Bobby and said, "Hey man. How are you doing, bro? Jesus loves you!"

He told me I needed to get some help. You see, our home was a 1978 single-wide trailer with a dilapidated basement underneath. The walls were paper thin, so he had heard every mean thing I said to Jackie and Destiny. He then listened to me change my tune as I brought up the love of Jesus. There was also a cut on my hand from punching a hole through the door, and I was still bleeding.

It was obvious I was a complete hypocrite! I really didn't want to be a hypocrite, but I couldn't help it. The problem was I had confessed Jesus and tried to incorporate Him into my life, but I had not *surrendered* my life to Him. Unless people fully surrender their lives to Christ, transformation will be in gridlock, and they will remain in a constant war within themselves, never fully becoming who they're called to be. Bobby remained friends with me and put up with my conversations about Jesus, especially since all of these talks ended with me smoking a joint. I continued taking bong hits, drinking, partying, and doing crack. He listened to Jackie and me argue about finances, and he knew that checks were bouncing because I was stealing her money to keep up with my drug use. Bobby knew I was an addict in every sense of the word. Time and time again he watched me say one thing and do another, but he stayed a loyal friend to me regardless.

Every Saturday morning there was a class at Dan's church called the Transformers Class, led by the elders of the church and based on Romans 12:2:

> And do not be conformed to this world, but be transformed by the renewing of your mind, so that you may prove what the will of God is, that which is good and acceptable and perfect.
>
> —ROMANS 12:2, NASB

No matter how hard I partied the Friday night before, I always managed to get myself to class on Saturday morning. I would go in straight off of a binge, with no sleep, smelling like weed and alcohol, and I would act like everything was OK. Dan was always so kind and patient with me. He only came to a few of these classes, so it was usually the elders leading the meetings. The elders, on the other hand, despised me for the sin I was living in and the front I was putting on for church. They knew I was on drugs, drinking, and lying about how things were truly going in my life, and they knew I wasn't married to the woman I was living with. Basically everything about me ruffled their feathers. I really wanted to change, but I didn't know how to, so I tried everything I could to hear the Word of God. I knew I needed to be at church. Every Saturday, rain or shine, I was there for class. You see, I saw a consistency in Dan that I had never seen before. So while all of this craziness was going on in my own life, I was seeing stability and real Christianity walked out in Dan's life. And even though the elders were upset with me, I recognized they were still men of God too, so I tried to honor them as well.

One night I drove out to go on another binge. I had completely run out of money, and I didn't have enough to buy crack. I stopped at the store to use a pay phone to call my dealer. He didn't answer, so I called another dealer and tried to get him to front me some drugs because I didn't have the money. It had been five and a half months since I had become a confessing Christian who incorporated Jesus, but I still didn't have any clue about who I was in Christ. After I hung up the phone, I turned around to leave. My girlfriend and my daughter were in the car right behind my Jeep.

Jackie shouted, "Look at what you've done to your daughter!"

My daughter was crying profusely and screamed, "Daddy, you promised!"

I said, "I know. I'm sorry." And I really was sorry, but I couldn't stop it. I was trapped in a Romans-7-lifestyle life, meaning I didn't want to do it, but I did it anyway. While I was doing it, I knew I shouldn't be doing it, but I continued to do it.

> For what I am doing, I do not understand; for I am not practicing what I would like to do, but I am doing the very thing I hate.
>
> —ROMANS 7:15, NASB

I hugged my daughter and told her I would come home, but as soon as I got in my Jeep and backed out, these voices in my head took over: "You need drugs, and you need them now!" Jackie and Destiny were in their car right behind me, so I spun out of the parking lot and took off down the streets of the city. They couldn't keep up with me and lost my trail. It was so sad. My life was all twisted and out of control because there was no relationship with Jesus. When I had originally started learning about Jesus, I opened the Bible multiple times. But I couldn't understand what I was reading, so I gave up trying to pursue a personal relationship with Jesus for myself. I was going to church and listening to the teachings, but my life was a total wreck because it wasn't fully surrendered to Christ.

Most self-proclaimed Christians fail to read their Bibles to get revelation, because they don't understand what they're reading. So they stop opening the Scriptures to glean for themselves, and instead they rely upon their pastors and teachers to explain it to them. Then their pastor becomes the middleman between them and God. This is really dangerous because they become a people who are always learning but never able to come to the knowledge of the truth.

Your pastor isn't meant to be your only source. You were made to have a relationship with Jesus yourself. Hypocrisy among professing Christians is the reason many people don't want to have anything to do with the church—and without a personal relationship with Jesus, hypocrisy is inevitable! I had no idea a personal relationship with Jesus was even possible or available to me. For months I had been living as a hypocrite, saying one thing and doing another. The very thing I hated, I had become.

The same night that I drove away from my wife and daughter, I went down a street in a part of town I normally didn't enter because it's so dangerous. My usual dealers didn't even live in this area, as it was known as a place where people get killed. But I was desperate and knew I could find what I was looking for somewhere along that street. I picked up a fifteen-year-old kid from New York City who was carrying drugs on him and convinced him to get into my car. He was hauling a bunch of crack cocaine, and I managed to get him to hand it to me to let me take a closer look at it. He put about a quarter of an ounce of it into my hand. Darkness entered my Jeep, and I could sense the evil of the moment—somehow I knew it was my last drug deal and my life could end because of it. You see, I didn't have any money to pay him, so I told him, "You have the right to remain silent. Anything you say can and will be used against you in a court of law." I read him his rights and told him I was a cop. Then I told him to get out of the car and put his hands on the hood.

As soon as he cleared the door, I released the clutch, put the car in gear, hammered the gas, and tore out of there! Immediately he spun around and fired a 9mm at my passenger-side window from about eight feet away. BOOM! BOOM! BOOM! BOOM! The deafening shock wave of blasts resounded throughout my vehicle as he continued to empty the clip. Right then I heard a voice like thunder: "I took those bullets for you. Are you ready to live for Me yet?"

Imagine the sound you'd hear standing under a roaring waterfall. That was what it sounded like! As the flash of shots resounded through the Jeep, this mighty voice reverberated over the gunfire and echoed straight through me with so much power, I felt as though I would die! But I knew the One speaking hadn't come to kill me—He had just saved my life!

Today I'm a radical Jesus lover who tells people about Him wherever I go, and some people think I am too extreme with my faith in the Lord. They say, "Todd, what's wrong with you?" Here is why I'm so extreme: I should be dead, and God didn't save me so that I could remain bound. He saved me so that I could represent Him in the earth. And He saved all of you for the same reason!

. Once I had escaped to a safe place out of the city, I smoked all the crack I had taken from that kid as fast as I could, and with every hit I took, that voice kept coming back, again and again, "I took those bullets for you. Are you ready to live for Me yet?" The voice wouldn't go away! It was ringing in my head. It was tormenting me from the inside out, and even though I took more than one hundred hits of cocaine, I couldn't get high the whole night! The cocaine was the real deal, and I knew the difference. I had taken more than enough hits to kill a person, but it didn't work. It was having zero effect on me! I was shaken to the core, as I knew it was all because of God. I finally headed home. I pulled into my driveway, got out of my Jeep, and took out my flashlight to inspect the damage. I looked all over the vehicle, and to my astonishment I couldn't find any holes from the bullets anywhere on the Jeep!

That kid had unloaded an entire clip at my vehicle at close range, and there wasn't even a nick left from a fired bullet! I knew it could only be the protection of God. Suddenly I remembered that a couple weeks earlier Dan and I had visited a place called Teen Challenge to consider the possibility of my going there. At that time, I wasn't willing to enroll because it reminded me of boot camp, but it was the first place that entered my mind after this terrifying experience. I just knew in my heart that I had to go there.

I walked to the door of our house, petrified because of all that had taken place. When I opened the door, my girlfriend was home. She told me she hated me and wanted me out of her life. I told her I would go, and I remember my daughter crying for me as I walked back out.

I had now lost everything.

Chapter 4

Total Surrender

I called Dan and told him everything that had happened. The day after I lost everything, he helped me get into Teen Challenge, a Christian rehabilitation ministry. They help not only teenagers but also adults and families with problems such as substance abuse and other self-destructive behaviors. Teen Challenge has an amazingly high success rate because they are Christ centered. Many people really get free and never return to their old lives after graduating from Teen Challenge.

However, they didn't have a bed for me right away, so Dan told me I could stay with him until a bed opened up.

That same day, I called my best friend, Bobby, trembling.

"Dude, last night I got shot at by some guy, and I heard God speak to me!"

"Todd, listen, haven't you shown by now that Jesus isn't real? You've been doing this thing for the last six months man, and nothing's changed."

"I'm telling you, He's real!"

"Bro, He's not real. The guy was just a bad shot."

"No, He is real!"

Then I told him I had made the decision to go to this rehabilitation center, and he was really happy and told me he was proud of me. However, his excitement quickly changed when I divulged that I was going to be learning more about Jesus.

He got really upset and said, "Why would you go away to learn about somebody that's not real?"

"He is real, man! You have to meet this pastor! Would you just talk to him?"

"I don't want to talk to a pastor! I know you! I don't care about a pastor. I care about you! You need to find the strength from within to fix yourself! If I can do it, so can you! Listen, man, it's better that you would open your mind and it would be better that you would go in there realizing that Jesus isn't real. Let them help you, man! You need help. I'll be here for you when you get back, and we'll jam!"

Then I explained that this wasn't a typical rehab program. Most rehab programs only last for a month. This program would last a full year, and there would be no contact allowed with him, even by telephone or letter.

He lost his composure. "What? A year? Why would you go away for a whole year to learn about something that's not real? You're throwing your family away! You're throwing your life away!"

"I've already lost my family. I've already lost Jackie. She doesn't want anything to do with me. And Destiny is so hurt, Jackie is not going to let me see her. I'm devastated."

"You need help, bro. I don't know what I'm going to do. You're my only friend."

"I can't have any contact with anyone for a full twelve months, but will you be here when I get out?"

"Yeah, man. You're my only friend!"

"Well, look, man, when I write music again, it's going to be all about Jesus."

He said, "Well, I don't know about all that, but I'll be waiting for you when you come home."

I told Bobby how much I loved him and asked if we could see each other one more time before I went to rehab, but he had his kids and wasn't able to see me before I went in. He told me he loved me, and we hung up the phone. Little did I know, that would be the last time I would ever speak with my best friend.

It took three days before a bed became available for me, and I was able to get into Teen Challenge. My daughter was really sad when she found out I was going away, but my girlfriend was very glad that I was getting out of her life. I had destroyed everything. I had charged up all of our credit cards, put us through bankruptcy, and ripped off her mom, her stepdad, my grandma, my grandpa, my uncle, my aunts, and my sisters. I ripped them all off! I had stolen from everybody. I was a thief and a quitter. I had quit everything except drugs. She was tired of it all and just couldn't deal with me anymore.

When I went into Teen Challenge, I had no idea what to expect. In thirty-four years I had never read through an entire book, because I had a reading comprehension disability. When I tried to read, I couldn't stay focused, my mind would wander off, and I would completely lose my train of thought. I couldn't retain the information I was reading. I could look up answers in a book, but I couldn't concentrate long enough to read through a book and still be able to remember what it was all about. So there I was, in this place that was going to teach me about the Bible, and yet I couldn't read! The good thing is the Bible is not only meant for the brain! The Word of God is meant for the heart! See, your heart can take you places your mind can never fit. You can't afford to just plug the Bible into your brain, because it's with the heart one believes unto righteousness! Your soul has the necessity to be renewed by the truth, which is communicated by the Holy Spirit to your spirit.

> If you confess with your mouth the Lord Jesus and believe in your heart that God has raised Him from the dead, you will be saved. For with the heart one believes unto righteousness, and with the mouth confession is made unto salvation.
>
> —Romans 10:9–10

After three days of being at Teen Challenge, my attitude had changed. I had been talking with Dan and had prayed and asked God to be Lord of my life. I said, "God, if You're real, show me that You're real, and I'll live for You." It was as simple as that!

Once I had submitted myself to God, I viewed everything differently. A switch had flipped, and I didn't have an attitude problem with authority! For my whole life before that, I always had a problem with authority. I was my own authority—"You don't tell me what to do!" At Teen Challenge they tell you what to do—big time! But when I fully surrendered my life to God, He became my complete authority, and I no longer had a problem with earthly authority. If they told me to go mop the floor, I said, "Yes sir," and mopped the floor.

Then I got called to the office for a phone call. The counselor there told me my pastor was on the phone. He told me to close the door and sit down. Do you know that look on someone's face when he has really bad news? Well, he had that look on his face.

Immediately my worst fears came flooding into my mind. I had been living in a constant state of fear and paranoia because I had ripped off all of those drug dealers from town, and we lived about six miles out of the center of the city. I thought for sure that someone had followed me home and killed my family.

"Is it my daughter? Tell me it's not my daughter! Is it my girlfriend? I know she hates me, but I can't stand the thought of anything bad happening to her!" I took the phone. It was Dan.

"Todd, you have to promise me something. Promise me you won't leave."

"What happened?"

"It's Bobby. Bobby had a brain aneurysm."

I didn't even know what a brain aneurysm was, but I screamed, "NO!" Dan said Bobby was in a coma and the doctors didn't expect him to come out of it. They didn't expect him to live. I threw the phone down and ran out of the office. I had to be alone! I passed by the front door, but I knew leaving was not the answer. Instead I turned and went up the stairs to the prayer room because it was the only place that I could be alone. My best friend was dying. I didn't have anything to give him. I had never given him anything but hypocrisy. So I went in the prayer room. When I went to shut the door behind me, this kid held the door and followed me in. His name was Micah, and he was what I call a fruit tester. He's the kind of guy who gets in your face all of the time. If I had still been in the world and had not already submitted to God, things would have gotten very ugly. Still, I was only three days into Teen Challenge, and my soul was full of hostility and turmoil because the only person who had stood by me through everything—the only friend I had left—was dying.

Micah got right in my face and said, "It's not that bad, man. Whatever it is, it's not that bad. You need to chill out! You're acting like a big baby! Deal with it."

That was a defining moment for me. It was the final straw. I had reached the end of myself. I was overwhelmed and completely broken. I screamed, "NO!" Suddenly the presence of the Holy Spirit came in the room, and a peace I had never felt before came in and physically knocked Micah back into the couch. I fell to my knees, and the peace of God rested upon me.

I heard a still, small voice say, "You're not going anywhere. You're safe. You're OK." All the hostility I was feeling dissipated.

Micah said, "What was that?"

I said, "I don't know, man, but I'm not angry." I began to cry and prayed, "God, I love You and just thank

You—because I know You're real." The physical, tangible presence of God came upon me and took away all my anger. From that day forward I wasn't angry. The Lord completely took away my anger! There was only peace. Ever since then I have learned how to continually walk in peace, and I don't have to chase drugs to get it. It's a peace that doesn't come from my external conditions. This peace resides in me from what God has done in my heart—He's transformed my heart and my mind.

I left the room to go downstairs to talk to the counselor. I told him something had just happened in the prayer room, and I didn't know what it was. All I knew was that I liked Micah now. He said, "Well, then something *amazing* happened to you!"

I stayed in Teen Challenge. Every morning I got up before everyone else and opened the Bible. I would pray, "God, this Word has to get in my heart. I'm not going away. I know this is the only thing that's going to change my life. I have enough understanding to know it is so amazing, and it's the only thing that has the power to fix me."

Dan had told me, "Todd, if you don't get your mind transformed, nothing changes. And if you don't seek righteousness, you'll never know that you've been made free." So I went after the word *righteousness* in the Bible, along with the words *redemption* and *the blood of Jesus*, and to this day, I've never gotten away from those words. The Scripture began to become clear to me.

One day at Teen Challenge the counselors were talking about trials, and they said that the Bible says to count it all joy when you face trials.

My brethren, count it all joy when you fall into various trials, knowing that the testing of your faith produces patience.

—JAMES 1:2–3

I spoke up in class: "You've got to be kidding me! There is no way a trial is ever joyful!" See, at every trial I had ever been in, I was always in an orange jumpsuit. I couldn't understand how someone could find being in a trial to be anything remotely close to a joyful experience. I determined that I was going to tackle understanding the Book of James and find out why trials are such a joy—because I was so done with being on trial! Early the next morning I went to the prayer room all by myself and started reading through the Book of James.

I said, "God, there's no way that trials can bring you joy."

He said, "That's because you've always been guilty. But you're not guilty anymore!"

Now obviously I had completely misinterpreted that verse. The trials in this passage are not legal trials in a courtroom but the difficulties and problems we encounter in life. But you know what's amazing? When God spoke to me about that verse, He didn't rebuke me for my lack of understanding and correct me with technicalities. Instead He met me right where I was and spoke to me with exactly what I needed to hear: "You're not guilty anymore!" What a patient teacher the Holy Spirit is.

Then I read verse 5, where it talks about wisdom:

> But if any of you lacks wisdom, let him ask of God, who
> gives to all generously and without reproach, and it
> will be given to him.
>
> —JAMES 1:5, NASB

I thought, "That's it! I don't have any wisdom! I'm
clueless!" It was as if the lights came on and I realized
wisdom was what I was lacking. I admitted that I lacked
wisdom, and when I asked God for wisdom, I asked in
faith, believing that He would give it to me. If we don't
ask for things in faith, then we are like the waves of the
sea, blown and tossed by the wind, and we can receive
nothing if we are double-minded.

> But let him ask in faith, with no doubting, for he who
> doubts is like a wave of the sea driven and tossed by
> the wind. For let not that man suppose that he will
> receive anything from the Lord; he is a double-minded
> man, unstable in all his ways.
>
> —JAMES 1:6–8

We can't afford to be double-minded. We must have
a single focus: Christ, and Him crucified, resurrected,
living in us; the hope of glory!

> For I determined not to know anything among you
> except Jesus Christ and Him crucified.
>
> —1 CORINTHIANS 2:2

God willed to make known what are the riches of the glory of this mystery among the Gentiles: which is Christ in you, the hope of glory.

—COLOSSIANS 1:27

As I received wisdom, everything started to make sense. I realized that the reason I had hated trials so much is because I had always been guilty, and then I heard the Lord say, "You're not guilty anymore." You can only face trials with joy if you're not guilty. My heart began to flutter with excitement! I was catching on! I was beginning to understand the Scriptures, and I became very excited because I knew God wanted to give me wisdom and revelation and the knowledge of Him!

. . . that the God of our Lord Jesus Christ, the Father of glory, may give to you the spirit of wisdom and revelation in the knowledge of Him.

—EPHESIANS 1:17

I had been devouring the Scriptures before, reading as much as I could, but without understanding. Now when I devoured them, the Word was coming alive to me! I started to ruminate on the things I had read before—everything was coming back to me with fresh clarity and understanding! It has been fifteen years, as of this writing, and I am still devouring the Word. For example, I'll be at the gym or on an airplane, and I will listen to the same chapter again and again and again. I listen to and read God's Word all the time. I eat it. I breathe it. I live it. Jesus said, "Eat My flesh; drink My blood." He wasn't just referring to Communion.

He who eats My flesh and drinks My blood abides in
Me, and I in him.

–JOHN 6:56

Two months into Teen Challenge my life had been
radically changing as I began to realize who I was in Christ.
Things were going well, and I received privileges allowing
me to walk across the street to a bench where I could
play my guitar. One of my friends from Teen Challenge
went with me and sat next to me on the bench while I
strummed away. We saw a homeless man pushing a cart
down the street. I shouted, "Hey, man, Jesus loves you!"

He came over to us and said, "I know how much He
loves me, but do you know how much He loves you?"
He took one look at my friend and told him, "You have a
demon in you, son, and I'm going to pray for you, and this
thing is going to leave you."

My buddy became outraged and hollered back, "I don't
have a demon! Who do you think you are?" I thought he
was going to hit the man, but he just stormed off and
went back across the street.

Now, this homeless man had a baseball cap and
swim goggles on his head and sneakers on his feet. He
was wearing army fatigues, and he had been pushing
a shopping cart down the main street. After my friend
left, he sat down with me and preached the gospel to me
from the Book of Ezekiel. Ezekiel was an Old Testament
prophet who foretold the coming of a Messiah King,
who would cleanse and unify His people under a new
covenant and transform them by giving them new hearts
and putting His very own spirit within them.

For I will take you from among the nations, gather you out of all countries, and bring you into your own land. Then I will sprinkle clean water on you, and you shall be clean; I will cleanse you from all your filthiness and from all your idols. I will give you a new heart and put a new spirit within you; I will take the heart of stone out of your flesh and give you a heart of flesh. I will put My Spirit within you and cause you to walk in My statutes, and you will keep My judgments and do them.

—Ezekiel 36:24–27

Then he went on to explain righteousness to me—the very thing I had been seeking. This man didn't even know that I was in Teen Challenge. In the natural I was just some guy on a bench with a guitar. How would he know anything about me? Yet he prayed over me and thanked me for blessing him with my music. I didn't really know how to play the guitar. I had just been strumming along. So I thanked him for praying for me, and then asked him why he was out on the street, pushing the shopping cart around.

He said, "Twenty years ago the Lord told me to pick up my cross and follow Him. So I sold everything I had, and I've been pushing this shopping cart across America from mission to mission, telling anybody who will listen to me about my King." He was sold out! I looked down into the shopping cart and noticed it was full of Bibles.

I walked back across the street in a daze. When I got across the street, some of the guys from Teen Challenge, who had been standing on the porch watching, were making fun of me because I had been talking with the homeless man. I said, "Hey, guys, we're supposed to love people. How could you make fun of him like that?" You see, in my heart I felt genuine love for this man. Suddenly they all looked across the street as if they had seen a ghost, then ran back in the building. When I turned around to look, the homeless guy had disappeared! We were all astonished, as there wasn't anywhere for him to go. The street was straight and about a mile long. He had simply vanished!

That night when I went to bed, I had an incredible dream. Previously, every night since I had arrived at Teen Challenge, I had horrific nightmares and night terrors. I had dreams of being chased by grisly monsters, with nowhere for me to go and nowhere for me to hide. I was so afraid that I would sweat profusely throughout the night, soak through my sheets, and wake up screaming in fear. The nightmares became so intense that while I was still asleep, I would physically run around the room, trying to get away from the demons terrorizing me in my dreams. Night after night my roommates witnessed this, but they didn't want to wake me up because they were afraid of what I might do. It was awful! In the daytime the enemy couldn't have me, but at night he would torment me to no end. Back then I didn't understand that once we have surrendered our lives to Jesus, our dream lives belong to Him as well. The Book of Job talks about the Lord using our sleeping hours to open our spiritual ears and impart warnings and instructions, but the enemy wants to rob us of every opportunity and avenue to hear from God—including in dreams.

> Indeed, God speaks once, or twice, yet no one notices it. In a dream, a vision of the night, when sound sleep falls on men, while they slumber in their beds, then He opens the ears of men, and seals their instruction.
>
> —Job 33:14–16, NASB

I didn't know that in deep sleep God wants to seal up warnings and instructions for me. I didn't understand it then, but I do now! The night after the homeless man prayed for me, I had my very first dream from heaven. I dreamed I was in a valley with steep walls, and just like the beginning of my typical nightmares, there wasn't anywhere for me to go—except this time I cried out to God for help. The walls were like cliffs, and there was green grass coming all the way down them. Then the walls began to shake, and I heard a voice say, "Do not fear. I will never leave you nor forsake you." I woke up one minute before my alarm went off, grabbed my Bible, and ran to the prayer room with urgency, as usual, to spend time with Jesus. Every day I feed on Him because I can't afford to not have a relationship with Him. I must have Him in my life every day. I can't afford to just be good at quoting Scripture and throw it at people without understanding what it means. I can't afford to read the Bible and not understand my value.

When I got to the prayer room, I opened my Bible. It opened to Psalm 23. As I was reading the psalm, which I had never read before, the words jumped off the page:

Even though I walk through the valley of the shadow of death, I fear no evil, for You are with me; Your rod and Your staff, they comfort me.

—Psalm 23:4, nasb

I realized then that it had been the Lord who had spoken to me in my dream. The next night when I went to bed, I had the exact same dream in the valley again. And again I woke up right before my alarm went off. I went down to the prayer room. When I opened my Bible, I opened it right to Psalm 23 again! The third night the same scenario played out in my dream, except this time there was a light that shone down into the valley, and I was afraid. It was Jesus. He put His hand on my shoulder and said, "I will never leave you nor forsake you. This addiction will never touch you again. Go home, and restore friends and family." I knew that the first relationship that needed to be restored was my relationship with my daughter—that's what hit me. I needed to tell her I was sorry.

Now, I had entered Teen Challenge with a year-long commitment, but Jesus had just told me to go home. I realize that this is controversial, and I risk being misunderstood at this point. Anyone can say that God told them to do this or that, and people have misused this claim in the past. I can only say that it is true in my case. Jesus told me to go home, and the truth of my claim shows in the fruit of my life and the reality of the freedom I've walked in for over fifteen years. Having said that, I believe it's imperative to state that outside of a direct word from the Lord, no one should leave a rehabilitation program early. Once a person has committed to enter a program, he or she should honor that commitment and follow through.

When I woke up in the morning, I started packing up my things. The other guys said, "What are you doing, man? Satan can disguise himself as an angel of light!"

I told them I understood, but it wasn't Satan. Jesus had appeared to me in the dream and told me to go home, so I was going. When I went downstairs to the office, the counselors became very upset with me. You know, I can honestly say that ever since I became a Christian, I haven't been offended or hurt by anybody. I have lived without offense for all these years. People think that is so unattainable because people have issues. But Jesus canceled my lifetime subscription to issues! Attitudes need to go. Life is short, so leave a legacy!

One of the counselors who freaked out had been through Teen Challenge four times, so when he saw me leaving, he thought I was leaving just as he did three times before. He was screaming at me, spitting mad. With tears in my eyes I said, "Listen, it's Jesus, man."

He said, "Just get out of here then! Get out on the front porch before everybody else gets polluted!" And I get it. I wasn't hurt or upset. How could I expect him to understand an encounter that he didn't have?

So I called Dan to ask him to come get me. Now, as Dan was my pastor, he had been granted permission to come visit me at Teen Challenge on a regular basis. He had been visiting every two weeks, observing my progress in my freedom from addictions and my relationship with the Lord. So, when I called Dan to ask him to come get me, he said, "Todd, is this God?"

I told him all about my encounters with Jesus, then he said, "I'm on my way!" I took all of my belongings out to the porch and waited. Dan pulled up in his truck about forty minutes later and asked me how I was doing. Then he went inside to talk to the counselors. They screamed at him as well. Dan didn't scream back. He doesn't scream at people because he is in love with Jesus. Then he came back out and said, "Come on. Let's get in the truck. Let's go." First we stopped by the church before we went back to my house. (I'll come back to what took place at the church a little later on in this story.) Then, on the drive to my home, Dan told me every reason why I was going to make it. He wasn't telling me all the things I needed to watch out for. He kept telling me the reason I was going to make it, and that reason was Jesus!

We drove to my house so I could apologize to my daughter, because for the first time, I realized what it's like to be a father. I had to tell my daughter that I was going to give her a dad. I could finally be a dad to her. I had never really been a dad. I didn't know what it was supposed to be like until I had an encounter with God my Father. See, Jesus is the way, the truth, and the life, and no one comes to the Father except through Him.

> Jesus said to him, "I am the way, the truth, and the life. No one comes to the Father except through Me."
>
> —JOHN 14:6

Without an encounter with the love of the Father, we would live life as orphans. But Jesus says to you, "Don't fear. I will not leave you as an orphan. I will come, and the Holy Spirit that is with you will be in you."

> I will ask the Father, and He will give you another Helper, that He may be with you forever; that is the Spirit of truth, whom the world cannot receive, because it does not see Him or know Him, but you know Him because He abides with you and will be in you. I will not leave you as orphans; I will come to you.
>
> —JOHN 14:16–18, NASB

That's a promise. When I said yes to God, I was no longer an orphan. But I needed to know the love of the Father. Once I had experienced the love of the Father, I was equipped to give it to my daughter.

When my daughter saw the truck pull up, she ran outside on the porch. I picked her up and told her how sorry I was for all the times I stole money and all the mess I had caused.

She said, "Daddy, stop. You're home!"

"No, I'm out, but I'm not home. I can't live here, baby. I love you with all my heart, and I'm going to show you a father you've never seen before. I didn't know how to be a dad before, but I had an encounter with God. I met Him. He lives in me. Look in my eyes."

"Daddy, I love you."

"I love you too, baby. Now listen, you need to hear me," and I cupped her face in my hands. "Daddy is sorry about all these things that I have done."

"Daddy, what things?"

I began to explain all the things I had put her and her mother through. She looked at me with a blank stare and a smile on her face. Then her mom came out on the porch. I stepped back and began to tell her how sorry I was for everything I had put her through.

She said, "I know you are. While you were away, I gave my heart to Jesus."

I said, "You're kidding me! Oh my gosh!" Then I explained that I couldn't live there. See, for the first time in my life I was truly clean. The blood of Jesus had washed my conscience, and I couldn't knowingly live with her unmarried because that would be a sin. And the real kicker was that the reason my daughter gave me the blank stare was because the blood of Jesus had supernaturally washed her memory, and she could remember nothing of what I had done or how I had acted before! She had no recollection of the severe trauma that she had witnessed and had been under her entire life. The blood of Jesus had cleansed her conscience of every dead work that her father did from the beginning! It was a sovereign move of God. Righteousness had not only impacted my life—it touched my kid as well! At seven and a half years old she had zero memory of anything bad I had done.

Chapter 5

A Vessel for Honor

When I returned home, I realized that my whole life had been tormented and completely manipulated by addictions because of selfish desires. I had been a manipulator, a liar, a stealer, a killer, and a destroyer. My whole life had been twisted, and now I was convicted by the way I had lived. When Jesus told me to go home ten months early, I went home, not to just move back in but to live a completely different life! See, I had ruined nine years of my girlfriend's life. I had ruined my daughter's life. Up to that point, I had ruined what it looks like to be a dad. Then I made a decision that there was no way I was going to be a slave to sin any longer. There was no way I was going to let it manipulate me and destroy my life any longer. I was so convicted of my sins.

The first thing I told my girlfriend was that I couldn't live there. She said, "I know. We need to be married." I was in shock! She wanted to marry me!

I looked at Dan and said, "We need to plan this."

He said, "You're not planning anything. I know she loves you, and I know you love her. I've been talking to her, and I've been talking to you. I know both of you understand what covenant is like, so we'll get you married on Sunday in between first and second service." You see, the whole time I had been away, Dan had been counseling Jackie and Destiny, sharing what righteousness and forgiveness mean. He also had been teaching them about God's design for family, what covenant means, and what God can do with a surrendered man's life.

That day on the porch my heart was pounding. So much was happening. My friend, the Holy Spirit was convicting me about everything: the way I had lived, the manipulation, the maneuvering, the drugs—all the stuff that I had done. I had really hurt people. Right away the Holy Spirit convicted me about all the junk that was in my house. I had bongs and bowls, roaches, seeds, grow lights, and pornography. I had a huge amount of trash inside of that home. So even though I knew I was not going to move back in until we were married, I could not stand the fact that all of that junk was in my house, because it had made my house dirty. Because of Jesus I was a vessel set apart for holy use. I was clean, and I wanted my family to be in a clean home. I turned to Dan and said, "I need to go into the house and take care of some things. Will you stay here and be with my girls for me?"

He said, "OK. Sure."

Therefore, if anyone cleanses himself from these things, he will be a vessel for honor, sanctified, useful to the Master, prepared for every good work.

-2 TIMOTHY 2:21, NASB

Now, I want you to understand, I was *not* cleaning those things out of my house because I was being tempted by them or because I felt guilty. Jesus had set me free from those addictions and had forgiven me of my past! I was no longer an addict, and I wasn't afraid I was going to sin. I was being convicted of righteousness by my Father. I wanted to get rid of the stuff because it no longer had anything to do with me now that I belonged to Him. I was seeing myself with fresh eyes through His righteousness, so those things had to go!

And when He has come, He will convict the world of sin, and of righteousness, and of judgment: of sin, because they do not believe in Me; of righteousness, because I go to My Father and you see Me no more; of judgment, because the ruler of this world is judged.

-JOHN 16:8-11

God was training my senses to know what had to get out of my life. Righteousness trains the senses to discern between good and evil. Milk is for babes, and solid meat is for the mature.

For everyone who partakes only of milk is unskilled in the word of righteousness, for he is a babe. But solid food belongs to those who are of full age, that is, those who by reason of use have their senses exercised to discern both good and evil.

-HEBREWS 5:13-14

So I went through my house with a big trash bag. I got rid of a whole life full of collected junk. The Lord enabled me to remember every nook and cranny where I had hidden things. When I got to my pornography collection, I realized how much of a slave I had been to sin. Lusting after women never made me a man; it made me twisted and put me in bondage. Jesus had crushed every chain, brought me out of sin, and set me free! He set me *completely* free! Some people say that you're always going to be tempted, and since God created women, sometimes you just feel that urge to look. I'm telling you, Jesus crushed that ungodly desire! Because outside of the covenant of marriage, it's not supposed to be that way! I'm trying to help you here. See, that day, God enabled me to do something called cleaning house, because God wants our houses to be clean. It's not because we have to; it's because we get to! You can make a choice to live in sin and compromise your life, but you can't have fellowship with God or other people.

> If we say that we have fellowship with Him, and walk in darkness, we lie and do not practice the truth. But if we walk in the light as He is in the light, we have fellowship with one another, and the blood of Jesus Christ His Son cleanses us from all sin.
>
> —1 JOHN 1:6–7

Your sin will always find you out because God sees it all. Oftentimes people say, "God, I surrender all." But then they crawl off the altar to sin because they think, "I need this." The thing is we don't need it. We just need Him! There is a place inside of relationship with Him where all of this other stuff just isn't appealing.

I went to my back closet where all my grow lights were from growing weed, and I threw all of them away. See, God wants our houses to be clean because we represent Him. If people can't see Jesus in you, then they won't want what you have. Your witness isn't a witness without Him. So I took all of the trash out to the backyard to put it in my burn barrel. Because there was so much trash, it wouldn't fit in the barrel. I went to the garage, got a sledgehammer, and returned to the barrel to make all the trash fit in there. It couldn't just sit there; I had to get rid of it. There was metal and glass, as well as a lot of paper because of the magazines. I knew that would help with kindling. But I needed something better. So I went back to the garage and returned with gasoline. I doused the trash with gasoline and set it on fire.

I was so convicted in my heart because God was now residing in me, and He does not share occupancy with anything! He is a jealous God. He wants all of you, not some of you. He doesn't want 98 percent of you; He wants 100 percent of you! There's no plan B; there's only one option. You're either for Him, or you're against Him. You either gather or scatter. There's no in between. We can't afford to incorporate Jesus into our lives instead of fully surrendering to Him. For me a full surrender was burning everything in that barrel. So I lit it, and as it went up in flames, I worshipped Jesus over my past. That past has never whispered into my life again. As of this writing, I've been free from drugs and pornography for over fifteen years—and not just the act of fantasy but also looking at a woman with lust. What would happen if every time Christian men saw a woman, they saw the beauty that God sees instead of undressing her with their eyes? This is what the gospel offers. This is what it looks like. It is not condemnation; it is holy conviction.

I remember that Saturday after I came home from Teen Challenge, I was really looking forward to staying up late to watch my favorite TV show, a comedy program called MADtv. I loved comedians because they could make people laugh, and the comedians on this particular show were my all-time favorite. Before going to Teen Challenge, I normally watched MADtv while taking bong hits and drinking beer. But since I had turned away from that lifestyle, I was now sitting down to watch my show with a bowl of popcorn and a soda. So I wasn't high or drunk, and I had a clean conscience before God that wasn't violated.

You see, there's a place you step into that's a violation of your conscience. It's a little different for each person. For example, some people consciences aren't violated when they drive five or ten miles over the speed limit, because most cops say that's OK. For me personally—having lived so many years as a lawbreaker and then radically changing into a Jesus-loving, law-abiding citizen—going over the speed limit violates my conscience, and I can't do it.

So my show came on, and right away, during the introduction music, I started feeling a little strange. The first comedian came on, and they were making fun of the president. For some reason it wasn't funny. I couldn't laugh. The next comedian came on, and they were making fun of even more people. It was much worse than the first act. I didn't think it was funny at all. In fact I turned the TV off and started crying. I couldn't figure out what was wrong with me. Right then the Lord spoke to me. He said, "I've given you My heart. You can no longer laugh at other people's expense."

I laid down with my face on the floor and cried my eyes out. I realized I had made fun of people my whole life, but it didn't hit me until right then. I realized my heart had changed so much that I couldn't bear to hear people put other people down. If Christians would obey that little nudge from the Holy Ghost and pay attention to any violations of their consciences, it would change everything they do. If Christians would think about whether something is acceptable and simply follow their convictions, their entire lives would radically change for the better. Jesus wants to instill in us a holy reverence for purity! When you stop to realize that sin grieves the Holy Spirit and hurts people, you don't want to sin, because you love God and you love people.

After I turned the TV off and had that moment with the Lord, I opened up my Bible and spent time in His Word. From that point forward, reading the Bible became my evening indulgence instead of the television. As I began to dive into the Word, revelation started flooding in. Jesus began to prune off all these other little things in my life that violated holiness. God wants to prune each of us so that we can maintain a clean conscience and live a life worthy of Him. If we allow Him to be Lord of our hearts and Lord over our consciences, we will live lives completely free of guilt, shame, and condemnation. Our lives will become abundant in peace, joy, truth, grace, and mercy! When we allow the cleansing power of the blood of Jesus to infiltrate our thought lives, we can see clearly.

The reason holiness has been so far away from the body of Christ is the purity of the church is in direct proportion to the condemnation level of the church. The way to get past condemnation and a guilty conscience is to have a Son conscience. But you can't have a Son conscience unless you believe that God is your Father. And you can't truly believe He's a God who is trustworthy unless you believe that His Word is the unadulterated truth; that He is for you, not against you; and that He wants to remove the sin from your life because He loves you so much. He wants you to walk in the light as He is in the light, because He wants to have fellowship with you!

> But if we walk in the Light as He Himself is in the Light, we have fellowship with one another, and the blood of Jesus His Son cleanses us from all sin.
>
> —1 JOHN 1:7, NASB

Do you know what the most common thing I hear brand-new believers say right after they get saved? They say, "I feel lighter!" The moment a person is born again, the bondage of sin falls right off. The finished work of the cross becomes real to people the instant they say yes to Jesus and are born again! Jesus is a burden lifter for all those who are weary and weighed down with burdens.

> Come to Me, all you who labor and are heavy laden, and I will give you rest. Take My yoke upon you and learn from Me, for I am gentle and lowly in heart, and you will find rest for your souls. For My yoke is easy and My burden is light.
>
> —MATTHEW 11:28–30

He said, "Come to Me." And when we go to Him, He lifts off all our burdens, forgives all our sin, and then says, "Now learn from Me." Notice He didn't say, "Go and learn from your pastor." There's nothing wrong with learning from your pastor, but your pastor can't lift the burdens off your soul, and your pastor can't be your only connection to the Lord. To be yoked is to be together. It's a direct connection between you and Jesus. We are called the bride of Christ because we are one, yoked together with the Lord. Being alone with the Lord for the purpose of being with Him and learning from Him means you will find rest for your soul. Nothing else outside of a personal relationship with Jesus will bring lasting rest to your soul.

When you come to the Lord in the secret place, have faith that He sees you there and that He hears you when you pray. Believe His Word, which says, "Your Father who sees in secret will reward you openly."

> But you, when you pray, go into your room, and when you have shut your door, pray to your Father who is in the secret place; and your Father who sees in secret will reward you openly.
>
> —MATTHEW 6:6

God is not hard to find. He said, "If you seek Me, you will find Me."

> And you will seek Me and find Me, when you search for Me with all your heart.
>
> —JEREMIAH 29:13

And when we seek Him in secret, He rewards us openly. With what? With Himself! The reward for seeking God in secret is receiving Him in the open.

Rest is what the world desires. When you first come to Jesus, you've tasted it, but when you learn from Jesus, you maintain it. The enemy of your soul is an accuser. If you don't maintain a consistent relationship with Jesus, the devil will bombard you and accuse you of all that junk from your old life. The devil is constantly speaking. The only way to gauge whether the Lord is speaking or the enemy is speaking, the only way to know whose voice it is you are hearing, is to know what God's Word says. If we don't know what God's Word says, we might confuse the source of the voice. The devil can't get away with deceiving someone who is grounded in the Word and God's righteousness. When your conviction of righteousness is amplified, the voice of past sin is diminished. There's no way for my hand to cause me to sin if my mind is consumed by righteousness, because my mind would have to premeditate it. If my mind is in love with God, it can't premeditate sin anymore. I can make mistakes but not willfully.

There's a difference between my knowing God loves me and actively making myself available to receive that love on a daily basis. Jesus paid the price for you to be reunited with your Father and receive His love directly through communion with Him, and God wants to lavishly give you His love every day in relationship with you.

> The grace of the Lord Jesus Christ, and the love of God, and the communion of the Holy Spirit be with you all. Amen.
>
> —2 Corinthians 13:14

Chapter 6

New View of Life

Sunday came, and we were so excited to get married between the first and second services! I was so happy! My daughter was so happy! My bride was so happy! Jackie's mother and stepdad, who were also there, were so . . . angry. Her mom said, "I cannot believe that she is marrying you! She is throwing her life away!" I couldn't expect her to understand. I knew there was a walk that needed to back up my talk.

I walked up to Jackie's stepdad and said, "Man, I just wanted to say thanks for coming."

He said, "Don't talk to me, you liar! You're a thief and a loser, and you don't fool me!" He said that right there in church at our wedding.

I looked at him with tears in my eyes and said, "You'll see."

I wasn't angry. I understood. I don't get hurt by people anymore. They don't know what they're doing, or else they wouldn't do it. People often get hurt in the church and say things such as, "They should have known better." However, shouldn't we know better than to allow ourselves to get hurt and offended? You see, people often hop from church to church because of offenses. They keep going around looking for love instead of becoming love and plugging in where it's needed! Hurts and offenses only hold people back in bondage and ultimately destroy them from the inside out.

Now, remember how I mentioned that Dan and I had first stopped at the church the day I left Teen Challenge? Well, I want to fill you in on what happened there too, because it's important. That day was a church workday. When Dan and I showed up, everyone was outside trimming trees, trimming bushes, mowing the lawn, weed whacking, and so forth, and I just wanted to go help out! Any chance I get to serve Jesus is exciting for me! However, Peter, the top elder of the church, was there. He had paid for me to go to Teen Challenge, and he wasn't exactly happy to see me roll up on the church property with Dan that day.

Now, before we arrived, Dan had asked me, "Todd, are you sure you want to go to the church? They are probably not thinking like you're thinking right now."

I said, "I'm sure. God loves me, man!"

He said, "Amen." He knew what might happen if I showed up, but I wanted to go and help, so he took me.

When we got out and walked up to where they were working, Peter said, "Todd, what are you doing here?" I started to tell him what Jesus had done, but he interrupted me. "Oh, don't tell me Jesus anything, Todd! You agreed to go away for twelve months, and here it is two months, and you broke your commitment!"

Both Peter and the head pastor informed me that they didn't want or need my help. Now, I'm not telling you this so you can lick your church wounds; I'm telling you this so you can be free. People are not your problem; you are. Peter wasn't my issue; I was—if I allowed his sin against me to produce sin within me.

Peter, being sarcastic, said, "It's OK, Todd. Why don't you just go on home and move back in with your girlfriend?"

I told him, "I can't." See, I had changed, but they didn't believe it yet.

The following Saturday there was a second church workday. I was back at the church again to help out.

> And whatever you do in word or deed, do all in the
> name of the Lord Jesus, giving thanks to God the
> Father through Him.
>
> —Colossians 3:17

I wasn't there to work on the church for them to thank me. I was there to work for the Lord, and I already had the thank-you—it's Jesus! Whatever I do, I do it as unto the Lord and not for people, so I don't need a thank-you from people. What does this look like for you? It may look like your being at your job and deciding to sweep the floor, whether or not your boss sees you or says, "Thank you." It may mean you do an excellent job on your report without expecting to be told, "Well done," or, "Congratulations!" Instead of saying to yourself, "Well, the boss didn't even care! I won't be doing *that* again," you say, "I didn't do this for the boss anyway. I am doing an excellent job because I'm doing this for the Lord!"

What if your boss wasn't the one responsible for your raises? What if *your giving* is? And what if your giving is responsible not just for your finances but your entire life! I'm talking about everything you are, from the top of your head to the bottom of your feet. You are an offering! You are a sweet aroma to the Father, a fragrant offering. Your life is an offering unto the Lord, a living sacrifice, holy and acceptable, which is your pleasing service unto the Lord.

> Therefore I urge you, brethren, by the mercies of God, to present your bodies a living and holy sacrifice, acceptable to God, which is your spiritual service of worship.
>
> —Romans 12:1, NASB

Everything about you is an offering to the Lord—your time, your service, your eyes, your ears, the way that you walk, the way that you talk, the way that you think. Everything about you belongs to Him. You need to have a one-track mind. The Bible tells us that if you sow to the flesh, you will reap corruption.

> For the one who sows to his own flesh will from the flesh reap corruption, but the one who sows to the Spirit will from the Spirit reap eternal life.
>
> —Galatians 6:8, NASB

All things are permissible but not all things are beneficial for you, so whatever you do with your time that isn't in tune with the Christian life or keeps you on idle is wasting the opportunity you have to learn and understand who you are in Him and who He is in you. That is the priority! Hobbies, sports, television—those things aren't bad in and of themselves, but your priority must be Him! Why would you spend your time sowing into something that is not furthering you in the kingdom?

> All things are lawful, but not all things are profitable.
> All things are lawful, but not all things edify.
>
> —1 CORINTHIANS 10:23, NASB

Why would I sit and watch a two-hour show on television that is going to make me regress and actually try to resurrect the old man? I want to raise the dead—but not *that* dead man! Your mind needs to be completely wrecked by the gospel! Don't believe the lie that you need time to unwind by watching an hour and a half of the evening news on television, as if that is somehow going to help you. This is especially destructive if you're failing to get the good news into your heart, because then all you hear is the bad news, and all you see is how bad things are, instead of hearing about all the good the Lord wants to do through your life amidst the bad things.

I'm not trying to give you rules; I'm trying to give you tools. Jesus wants to make you manifest what goodness looks like! Whether you're a guy or a girl, married or single, a parent or not, young or old—whoever you are and whatever you do—you're important! There are no unimportant people! You can praise God while you're doing another load of laundry—as you turn your kid's shirt right side out, you can pray, "God, I thank You that You are turning my kids' right side out!" or "God, I'm doing this as unto You! God, I thank You as I'm doing another load of laundry; I thank You for the privilege of loving my family. You're amazing. Thank You, Father!" Everyone's life is equally valuable.

That Saturday when they rejected me, I went around front and got a broom. No one was watching me, not even Dan, and I swept the sidewalk, just crying and thanking Jesus. You see, some people say they don't go to church because they got hurt at church. They really just got hurt by people, and neither the hurt ones nor the ones who did the hurting knew who they were in Christ when the offense happened.

> For our struggle is not against flesh and blood, but against the rulers, against the powers, against the world forces of this darkness, against the spiritual forces of wickedness in the heavenly places.
>
> —EPHESIANS 6:12, NASB

It all comes back to your identity in Christ. When we all stand before the Father, no one will have an excuse as to why they didn't burn for Jesus. You will find that every reason for growing cold was all just an excuse because you didn't understand who God created you to be. You see, once you understand the price that heaven paid for you, then you'll understand that the cross isn't just the revealing of your sin—the cross is also the revelation of your value! Something underneath all of your sin had to be very valuable for heaven to have gone bankrupt just to get you back!

The very people at my church who couldn't stand me taught this amazing class on Saturdays that I wanted to attend so I could grow and learn. It didn't matter how they treated me. I still realized I had something to learn from them. See, if people treat you wrong, it doesn't mean you can't learn from them; it just means they help perfect you in love! Oftentimes it's the people who are the angriest with you that help perfect love in you. Some people would say, "Well, Todd, I just don't have the patience for that." You know, if we held a conference on patience, not very many people would show up. A lack of patience is just a lack of love. The Word of God says, "Love is patient." In fact it is the first description of love in 1 Corinthians:

> Love is patient, love is kind . . .
> —1 Corinthians 13:4, nasb

You'll never get to love without patience because trials, fires, and trouble produce patience. Patience produces character, and character produces hope.

> Tribulation produces patience, patience produces character, and character produces hope.
> —Romans 5:3–4, mev

You can't go through fire the right way unless you're already on fire! How would you like to be perfect and complete, lacking nothing? It's not a trick question. It's in the Bible! God's Word says in the Book of James that trials produce patience, and to let patience have its perfect work in you so that you may be perfect and complete, lacking nothing.

> My brethren, count it all joy when you fall into various trials, knowing that the testing of your faith produces patience. But let patience have its perfect work, that you may be perfect and complete, lacking nothing.
>
> —JAMES 1:2–4

The Transformers class at my church was on the topic of transformation and was based on Romans 12:2.

> And do not be conformed to this world, but be transformed by the renewing of your mind, that you may prove what is that good and acceptable and perfect will of God.
>
> —ROMANS 12:2

Now, the elders who were teaching the class didn't believe that I was for real. They didn't believe that a true transformation had taken place in me, especially since I had left Teen Challenge early. You see, Peter owned a slate roofing company, and he believed in giving anyone a chance. It didn't matter what kind of criminal history you had or if you had been to jail. He would give anybody one fair chance. So Peter had hired me before I ever entered Teen Challenge. In fact, four days into the job, I called in sick just so I could go to his house and steal the copper I knew was in his garage—except the Lord convicted me, and I couldn't go through with it. Instead I went to his front door and told his wife that I had come to steal from them, but I had been convicted and couldn't go through with it. Obviously Peter fired me that day, but even after he fired me, he still covered the cost for me to go to Teen Challenge. It cost $700 per month, and he had committed to pay for my entire year. By the time I walked out of Teen Challenge, he had already spent $1400 for me to be there.

When I went to class, he said, "Todd, why are you here?"

I replied, "Because I want to learn from you guys!"

"Why would you want to learn from us? You didn't stay at Teen Challenge, and you didn't follow through, and you didn't . . . " He went on and on.

"I'm here because I need to grow!"

"You're right! You need to grow—but why do you think it's here?"

"Because you guys know a whole lot more than I do, and I know that I can learn from you."

"OK," he said. "Just be quiet!"

When we were in class, Peter would ask questions, and I would raise my hand when I had an answer burning inside of me. But he often called on someone else. Occasionally, when he could no longer ignore me, he would let me answer, then tell me it was the wrong answer—even though in my heart I thought it was right. I still wrote down whatever answer he gave me. I was the thorn in his flesh. I woke up early every Saturday to go to the class. I would ask if I could help with anything.

The answer was always no. "Todd, you're not even at a kindergarten level of maturity! We cannot let you help do anything."

"Well, can I at least dump the trash?"

"NO!"

I continued to faithfully go to class and learn as much as I could from the Word of God. The Bible was the first book I could understand because as I read through it, I asked the Lord to help me become it. So the Lord had me meditate on Ephesians chapter 1 for a full year. I learned that God had cleaned my conscience in order for me to serve Him. The reality of my right standing with God is that old things have passed away, and all things have become new. I was a brand-new person, one who had never existed before, a brand-new creation in Christ!

> Therefore, if anyone is in Christ, he is a new creation; old things have passed away; behold, all things have become new.
>
> —2 Corinthians 5:17

My daughter now had a father whom she could see worshipped Jesus at home and in public. My wife now had a husband who didn't change into someone else when he got home. I'm in love with God every day, 24/7, which means there's no change in me whether I'm here or there. See, we are made in the image of God, and with Him there is no change, or turning, or shifting of shadows, so with us there should not be any change either.

Every good gift and every perfect gift is from above, and comes down from the Father of lights, with whom there is no variation or shadow of turning.

—JAMES 1:17

We should not give strength to the weakness of the flesh. We should give strength to the strength of God's Spirit because it's not by might, nor by power, but by His Spirit:

Then he said to me, "This is the word of the LORD to Zerubbabel saying, 'Not by might nor by power, but by My Spirit,' says the LORD of hosts."

—ZECHARIAH 4:6, NASB

The reality of God's righteousness puts me in right standing with the Lord. I'm so in love with Jesus that if anything tries to violate that right standing, the Holy Spirit just cuts it right off!

As I mentioned before, my best friend, Bobby, had a brain aneurysm while I was still at Teen Challenge. He was in a coma and on life support, and the doctors weren't hopeful for his recovery. The day after Jackie and I got married, I felt led to go see Bobby because the Lord had spoken to my heart. When I arrived at the convalescent home where Bobby was staying, his wife was there in the room at his bedside. To walk in that room was one of the hardest things I've ever done. Bobby was hooked up to all kinds of machines, his brain was swollen, and his skull was cut away. I was heartbroken. I turned to his wife, Betty, who was not a Christian, and I apologized for not representing Jesus well to Bobby.

She said, "Jesus? Really? Jesus? Look at my husband!"

I said, "I'm sorry."

She told me to shut up; then she went over to the corner and sobbed bitterly.

I looked at my friend, who was lying there, dying. At that point in my life, I did not understand healing. All I knew was that for five and a half months I was the only guy who had the opportunity to represent Jesus to him—but I didn't. And now I was sitting with him, there on his deathbed. I could speak to him, but he couldn't hear me—he wasn't even home. I kept telling him how sorry I was. For a short period of time all of my hypocrisy passed before my eyes—all the partying I had done with Bobby, getting high, referencing Jesus here and there, but my actions never reflecting Jesus at all. It was heavy condemnation. Then suddenly God took it from me. I said, "I'm sorry, man. I love you, man! Jesus is real! Bobby, if you can hear me, pray with me!" But he couldn't because he wasn't home. It seared my heart.

Life is short! You know, there are people who know you who aren't Christians. Let me ask you something:

Do they see Jesus in you?

Does your life exemplify the gospel?

Does your life exemplify hypocrisy?

Are you just apathetic?

Life is short! You're here to leave a legacy!

The next morning Betty called to tell me that Bobby had died. My heart was crushed to pieces. I held my wife close, and we both cried together. Betty said that I was

Bobby's one and only friend, and he would have wanted me to speak at his funeral. The night before the funeral I was a total wreck. When I showed up to the funeral home the next day, Bobby's two young children were standing by the coffin, saying, "Daddy! Daddy, wake up!" It was just horrible! This guy was a husband, a father, and my best friend, and my heart was totally cut to pieces.

When it was time for me to go up front to speak, Bobby was in the casket behind me. The Lord had given me a poem to share about friendship and what it means to be a true friend. A friend stands by you and never leaves; a friend lays down his life. That's a true friend! I had confessed Jesus to Bobby, but I had nothing to back it up, so he didn't see Him in me. Some of his last words to me were, "I don't believe in Jesus, but I believe in you." I had to tell his kids that I didn't know where their daddy was. I explained that there were only two places we could go when we die, heaven or hell. I was broken because of my hypocrisy. Bobby had a chance to see who Jesus was, but I didn't walk it out. Again, life is short! You are here to leave a legacy!

We need to fully and completely give our lives to the King. There are people dying every day! Let me ask you this: How is your walk with Jesus? Do the people around you believe that you believe the things you say you believe, or do you walk out something different? When someone makes fun of someone else, do you join right in, or do you take a stand? How about when you're in line at the grocery store and people complain about the cashier because she's a little slower than you want her to be? Do you say, "Yeah, they should put someone else over here," or do you stand up for her and say, "Hey, you know, she really needs grace. I say we pray for her right now"? This is how I live my life, guys! I live with a burning, passionate desire every day to walk out this gospel so that nobody who encounters my life is going to have any doubt that Jesus is real! The gospel shouldn't be known merely by its doctrine. It should be known by its passionate heart's cry! It should be known by a burning desire for people around you to know Him. We should be known as a people without hypocrisy or compromise. Those who have submitted to God have given themselves completely to God, 100 percent! Listen, I love you, but I won't water down this message for anyone!

Everywhere I go I see people come to Jesus. Everywhere I go I tell people about Jesus. I went in a drugstore recently to get some eye drops. I asked the lady behind the counter how she was doing, and she told me her day was so long. So I said, "Give me your hands, honey." I prayed with her and told her, "God loves you so much."

She started trembling and said thank you. See, we have something to give the world! Why hold it back any longer? Why hold on to yourself? Why not give yourself completely to Jesus? He is amazing! He paid the ultimate price for you—not only to get you to heaven but to have heaven flow through you so that you can destroy the works of the devil for a living. How awesome is that?

He who sins is of the devil, for the devil has sinned from the beginning. For this purpose the Son of God was manifested, that He might destroy the works of the devil.

He didn't pay a price for us to play the hypocrite or play the harlot! Hot or cold? Choose one! Don't be lukewarm, but burn with passion!

I know your deeds, that you are neither cold nor hot; I wish that you were cold or hot. So because you are lukewarm, and neither hot nor cold, I will spit you out of My mouth.

−REVELATION 3:15–16, NASB

Be fiery about this thing! Don't sit back and hold Jesus back. Don't go to your family reunion and be too ashamed to mention the name of Jesus. Everywhere I go, I get to give this to people. Every time I travel, I know I'm going to be locked in a steel tube at 36,000 feet with people who need to know what I have. I won't be silent about Jesus! I am consumed with a passionate fire for Jesus! I am consumed with a passionate fire from heaven. How could you not want to be like this? I would ask you this day, church: Considering most of you have a Bobby in your life, someone who doesn't know God, are you living and walking in such a way that your Bobby is going to know Jesus, or are you compromising? Christianity isn't a secret mission! We are lights in a dark world. We are to live Jesus out loud. Some would say, "That's a private matter. I don't like to talk about Him in public." That's nonsense! Take the basket off of your head and run with Jesus!

. . . so that you will prove yourselves to be blameless and innocent, children of God above reproach in the midst of a crooked and perverse generation, among whom you appear as lights in the world.

—PHILIPPIANS 2:15, NASB

No one, after lighting a lamp, puts it away in a cellar nor under a basket, but on the lampstand, so that those who enter may see the light.

—LUKE 11:33, NASB

You are the light of the world. A city set on a hill cannot be hidden.

—MATTHEW 5:14, NASB

Like I said before, resistance of the devil is a one-step program. When we submit to God, the devil is resisted. We don't just pick a fight with the devil. If we aren't submitted to God, we are fighting a losing battle.

Therefore submit to God. Resist the devil and he will flee from you.

—JAMES 4:7

When we submit to God, we resist the devil, and he flees! Why does he flee? Because you are submitted to God! He doesn't just flee because you command him to get away from you. He actually likes that because then he can get people frustrated, worried, and even terrified when he doesn't leave. The devil keeps saying, "So what?" Stop listening to him! Learn and understand the

Shepherd's voice, and then when that other voice comes, it's just a stranger's and you'll know not to follow:

But he who enters by the door is the shepherd of the sheep. To him the doorkeeper opens, and the sheep hear his voice; and he calls his own sheep by name and leads them out. And when he brings out his own sheep, he goes before them; and the sheep follow him, for they know his voice. Yet they will by no means follow a stranger, but will flee from him, for they do not know the voice of strangers.

–John 10:2–5

The voice of Jesus is the voice of truth. Every day, I wake up the same way, no matter what I face. It doesn't matter what I'm up against; it doesn't matter what trials I'm facing. Trials are there to help me with my faith. The devil wants to use trials to derail us, but trials are there to purify our faith so that we can increase in faith!

Consider it all joy, my brethren, when you encounter various trials, knowing that the testing of your faith produces endurance. And let endurance have its perfect result, so that you may be perfect and complete, lacking in nothing.

–James 1:2–4, nasb

Beloved, do not think it strange concerning the fiery trial which is to try you, as though some strange thing happened to you; but rejoice to the extent that you partake of Christ's sufferings, that when His

glory is revealed, you may also be glad with exceed-
ing joy.

—1 Peter 4:12–13

We cannot consider it a joy to face a trial if we are
not in Him when we go through them. When you're in
Him and you go through trials, He will crush those trials,
and you will see your growth and maturity. There is no
growth and maturity without trials. So many times we
beg God to get us out of a trial because we can't handle
it anymore. Our perseverance is thrown out the window.
There has to be something different about Christian
men and women of God so that when people see them
going through trials, they say, "Something is different
about you! What is this that you have?" People at your
workplace should say, "What is this hope that you have,
because I'm really struggling, man. How do you have so
much hope?" The Bible says that if someone asks about
your hope as a believer, you should be ready to explain it.

But sanctify Christ as Lord in your hearts, always
being ready to make a defense to everyone who asks
you to give an account for the hope that is in you, yet
with gentleness and reverence.

—1 Peter 3:15, nasb

Prayer of Repentance

Right now you could be feeling as if you haven't lived your
life the way you need to. There's only one way to change

this, and that's through repentance. If you will pray with me, God can change your heart, along with the way that you think. God can begin the transformational process of His authentic grace. He will begin to put His fear in and upon you so that you stop sinning against Him. Remember, up until this point it has not been possible to make any change in the way you've been living your life because you haven't obeyed or sensed a strong conviction to do so by the Holy Spirit. Now is the time—don't waste another moment of your life living this way. Other people's eternity depends on your living a pure life of devotion to Jesus! The Father will remove those things that make other people stumble so that you never have to have a Bobby in your life, so that the people who watch your life will see significant change, and so that everything regarding Jesus will be completely and overwhelmingly obvious to everyone who watches your life—because your life will look like Jesus. Pray with me now.

Lord God, I'm asking You to forgive me for sinning against You and wipe away the stain of hypocrisy that I have shown the world around me. Help me to live a godly life. Holy Spirit, I am asking You to show me what it truly means to live and walk in the fear of the Lord. Father, I ask that Your Word would be the foundation of my life. I pray the Holy Spirit would help me understand the truth that is in Your Word. You are my Father, and I ask You to teach me and help me know You more so that I can display You and all of Your glory and goodness to the world around me. Please forgive me and wash me clean. Please open my eyes and my ears so that I can see the way You see and hear the way You hear. Help me respond in a godly manner, and help me live my life fully ablaze with the gospel of Jesus Christ. Lord, thank You. Your Word says that I have been washed clean because I have confessed to You, and You are faithful and just to cleanse me of all unrighteousness. I thank You that the only thing that is left is righteousness, because I am the righteousness of God that's in Christ Jesus. Amen.

Prayer of Salvation

If you don't know God as a Father and you don't know Jesus Christ as your Savior and your Lord, I want to invite you to take this life-changing step that would allow Jesus to become everything to you. It's as simple as repentance and asking Jesus to take the life that really doesn't belong to you—your own life. All God is asking you to give up is what you were never created to be. You were never created for you. Then you can finally step into who you were created to always be—a son or daughter of the Most High God, your Father. Pray with me now.

Lord, I'm asking You right now, in the name of Jesus, to forgive me of all my sin. I have not only sinned against people, but I have sinned against You. I have broken Your holy laws. I am truly sorry from the depth of my being. I truly believe that Jesus was crucified for my sins and was raised for my justification so that I could be right in Your sight. The Bible says that the blood of Jesus washes my sins away. Please, Lord, I ask You to show me my created value and to help me understand why I'm on this earth. Jesus, I believe that You are the only way for me to get to the Father and have a relationship with the Father. Heaven will be my destination, but learning how to destroy hell every day as I remain here on earth will be my mission. Father, I thank You that the blood of Jesus cleanses me from all unrighteousness and all sin. I put my faith in the blood of Jesus right now. The Bible says to confess with my mouth and believe in my heart that Jesus is Lord and I will be saved. Lord, right now I confess and believe that Jesus Christ is Lord, and I am asking You to rescue me, deliver me, heal me, and set me free. God, You are amazing, and I love You. From this day forward I will honor You with my whole life and everything that I am. Father, I thank You for making Your home in me. I invite the Holy Spirit right now to baptize me with His presence and His person. You said in Your Word that You would never deny anyone who asks You for the gift of the Holy Spirit. So I ask You, Holy Spirit, fall upon me, come upon me right now, in the name of Jesus. Amen.

Chapter 7

Walk the Talk

One day I was looking through the paper and saw a job advertisement that said, "Pipe Layers Needed." It said experience was necessary, so I prayed, "God, You've got all the experience I need. I believe You can show me and teach me anything! If I lack wisdom, You'll give it to me . . . That's experience!" Now, understand that this was my first real job opportunity, in the sense that this time I was actually serious about getting a job and providing for my family. Before I got saved, I had no real work ethic, but after the Holy Spirit had revealed who I was in Christ, I realized my work was for the Lord, not for people.

And whatever you do in word or deed, do all in the name of the Lord Jesus, giving thanks to God the Father through Him.

—COLOSSIANS 3:17

I called Jackie to tell her about the job opportunity. She worked as a front desk manager at a hotel, so she accepted applications and hired people all the time.

I said, "Jackie, I saw an ad in the paper saying, 'Pipe Layers Needed.' What do you think about that?"

"Well, that depends. Are they looking for experience?"

"Yeah, it says, 'Experience necessary.'"

"Well, honey, what that means is you have to understand what the job is before you go. You've had to have done the job before. If I need to hire a night auditor with experience, I wouldn't just hire someone who doesn't know how to do it. I would need someone who already knows what they're doing so I don't have to train them."

"Yeah, but I think God is going to give me this job, and He knows everything! God is going to give me wisdom!"

"Honey, I think you should look for another job."

"Yeah, but this one pays really well, and we need that!"

"Well, you can try!"

So I called them on the phone, and the lady asked if I had any experience. I said, "No, but God is going to give me experience. My Father knows everything."

She said, "Who's your Father?"

I said, "God."

She said, "OK, you may fill out an application, but they are looking for people with experience."

I was so excited! I went to the office to fill out the application, and being a Christian now, I told the whole truth and nothing but the truth on the application.

Felonies?

"Oh yeah!"

Misdemeanors?

"Yep!"

I also added that I had been kicked out of the Marine Corps, extradited across America twice, wore the orange jumpsuit and shackles, etc. My story took up all the space on the front and back of the job application.

Job history?

"Oh, lots of jobs–that I left, quit, or was fired from."

See, I had never told the truth before, and now I was honored to represent Jesus in truth. I filled out everything on the application. It was the first time I told the whole truth on my job application. When I got to the end, I prayed, "God, thank You so much." I was so grateful for the work He had done in my heart that enabled me to tell the truth in its entirety.

You see, if you lie to get a job, then you have to live a lie to keep it, and I was done living a lie. I handed my application to the woman behind the desk. She looked at it and said, "Oh my!" And then she was speechless.

I told her that Jesus loves her and has a plan for her life.

She finally said, "OK, sir. Thank you. You may go. We'll call you."

I went home and told my wife that I had filled out the application and told the whole truth about all of my past.

"No!" she gasped. "Did they ask you for the whole truth?"

"No, but I have never told the truth before! It's going to be amazing! God is going to get me this job! He's going to open the door for me!"

"Honey, you're never going to get a job!"

"Do you want the man that used to lie back?"

"No."

Three days later I received a phone call at my house from the pipe-laying company. It was the same lady. I said, "Hey, I knew you'd be calling me!" I told her it was amazing that she was calling.

She said, "Yes, it really is surprising. They want you to come in for an interview."

I went in that same day. Before I left to go on the interview, Jackie warned me not to mess it up. I said, "How could I mess it up? I've already told them everything."

When I walked in, I immediately told them how excited and thankful I was for their giving me this opportunity. They were laughing and told me to settle down. They said they were laughing because of my application. As we went over my history, I shared all about how Jesus had changed my life. They told me they were looking for an experienced pipe layer, but they had never seen an application like mine before in their entire lives! So they decided to give me a shot because they didn't have anything to lose. They said I could start the following Monday. I was overwhelmed with joy! I told them I wouldn't disappoint them because I was working for Jesus.

When I came out of the interview, I called Jackie. "Honey, I went in for the interview."

Right away she said, "That's OK. There are other places hiring."

I said, "Honey, you don't understand. They gave me the job."

"Oh my gosh! You're kidding me! That's amazing!" she screamed. "When do you start?"

"Monday morning!"

She began crying tears of joy. You see, that phone call was a big deal because I had never given a dime to my family. In nine years I had never brought home a single paycheck—not even one. I had manipulated her and made excuse after excuse for why I couldn't hold a job. I was so excited because I could finally be the breadwinner my family deserved.

When Monday came around, I went into work full of zeal! It was 5:20 in the morning, and all the guys were gathered around the room, drinking coffee and getting ready for the day. Right out of the gate I got everyone's attention and said, "Hey guys! I just want to tell you all that Jesus loves you so much!"

They started jeering and cussing me out, asking who I was and why I thought I could talk to them. I told them I was the new guy, and that it was my first day. They told me to get away from them. I said, "Jesus loves you anyway."

Then I went to the office window, where a lady gave me a hard hat for the jobsite. Right then a guy walked by, and I noticed he had marked up his hard hat with all of his favorite bands. So I asked the lady if I could write on my hat too, and she said, "Sure, just don't put curse words on there."

I grabbed a permanent marker and wrote "Jesus Loves You!" "You're Amazing!" and "Helmet of Salvation," along with Scripture verses all over my hard hat. Then a guy named Tony came to pick me up in the truck.

When we arrived at the jobsite an hour later, I met Scott, my foreman. He said, "Are you the new guy? Nice hat."

I told him I was going to do an amazing job for him.

He said, "Finally! They send me somebody with experience!"

I said, "Oh no, I don't have any experience. I'm going to do an amazing job for you because I'm not working for you; I'm working for Jesus!"

He told me to shut up and get away from him.

All of my coworkers and I piled into the back of the truck. I was sitting next to this angry sixty-one-year-old man named Elwood. Elwood hated Christians. Five years earlier a Christian man went into his home, told him about Jesus, then convinced him to invest in his "Christian" company that was selling a product. The man told Elwood that the investment was so safe, even if something went wrong with the finances, he would still be able to recoup much more than he invested. So Elwood gave him around $75,000, which was all of his family's savings. When a hard time came, Elwood tried to get some money out of that fund, but he couldn't get it because the guy had disappeared. The whole investment pitch had been a scam. Elwood had no choice but to sell the family farm. This man had gone to Elwood's home, preached the gospel to him, then deceived him on purpose, causing him to lose all of his savings, his dairy farm, and any hope of early retirement. So Elwood's view of Christians was not good, to say the least. In fact most of the men there had a negative view of Christians based on witnessing their hypocrisy and poor conduct.

Do you know what happens when you tell someone you're a Christian? You're now on high observation mode. People are just looking at your life, waiting to see what that actually means. Do you know that we are to let our conduct be honorable among nonbelievers? Do you know that we are supposed to let our light shine?

Only let your conduct be worthy of the gospel of Christ, so that whether I come and see you or am absent, I may hear of your affairs, that you stand fast in one spirit, with one mind striving together for the faith of the gospel.

–PHILIPPIANS 1:27

Let your light so shine before men, that they may see your good works and glorify your Father in heaven.

–MATTHEW 5:16

We are not supposed to be basket heads, right? We are supposed to let our light shine! So those guys at work, who had been hurt by people claiming to be Christians and had such a bad view of Christians, were seeing me there, proclaiming Jesus from my mouth, on my hat, and by my conduct. And conduct is the most important because what you confess means nothing if your life, your conduct, and your attitude aren't honorable. You are what you believe, not what you say. When what you believe becomes so strong in you that it begins to manifest in your life, Christ in you is what will manifest in your life all the time!

Every day the guys at work mocked me for my faith in Jesus, making fun of me, talking trash, and saying vile things to me, but I didn't break. Every day I went in, worked hard, loved them, and talked about Jesus. The Word of God says the power of life and death is in the tongue.

> Death and life are in the power of the tongue, and
> those who love it will eat its fruit.
>
> —Proverbs 18:21, nasb

If you allow the words coming out of someone else, unless that someone is the Lord, to influence the words coming out of you, then you are allowing yourself to be manipulated. You are the light. You are the good influence. If you are the only Christian at your job, please don't pray and ask God to get you out of there. You belong there!

> You are the light of the world. A city set on a hill can-
> not be hidden.
>
> —Matthew 5:14, nasb

You're supposed to be the light in the darkness. Christ in you is the hope of glory. Christ coming out of you is that hope being made manifest.

> . . . to whom God willed to make known what is the
> riches of the glory of this mystery among the Gentiles,
> which is Christ in you, the hope of glory.
>
> —Colossians 1:27, nasb

Christ in you is the influence they need around them! It is kingdom leaven, and a little leaven leavens the whole loaf—it infiltrates every place.

> Another parable He spoke to them: "The kingdom of heaven is like leaven, which a woman took and hid in three measures of meal till it was all leavened."
>
> —MATTHEW 13:33

The inside of our job trailer was covered in posters of naked women. There was pornography plastered on every wall. This is sadly typical of a construction worksite, but it was no longer typical for me. So I separated myself from the pornography because the Bible says to be separate from what is unclean. See, I can't be a witness if condemnation still remains in me, because then I have the same junk in my life that they're dealing with, and my witness becomes invalid. However, being free from that bondage means I can now be an effective witness for the Lord.

> Come out from among them and be separate, says the Lord. Do not touch what is unclean, and I will receive you.
>
> —2 CORINTHIANS 6:17

The guys taunted me and teased me about why I wouldn't look at the wall. I said, "Why would I look at that? I love my wife, and I'm happily married." I never said anything to shame my coworkers; I just spoke the truth in love. A lot of Christians unfortunately separate themselves from people when they are really supposed to separate themselves from the sin. We hate sin, but we love people. We can literally love people into the truth when we live a life free from sin and lead by example.

The other workers and I each had different duties to perform when we laid pipe on a property site. The excavator would dig out a deep trench for the pipe to go across. Then I would go down in the trench box, pull the pipe in place, and gauge how level it was by lining it up with a laser and setting it with stone underneath until it was perfectly level. That way, there would be no dips in the pipe that could cause problems later. Once I lined everything up and set it just right, I would sit at the end of the pipe and wait the four minutes it took for the other guys to fill in the dirt along the pipe before it got to my end. When they reached my end of the pipe, it was time to move so that they could fill the rest in, and then we would do it all over again. I used every bit of those four-minute intervals to read a tattered little New Testament I kept with me at work. I had become disciplined and militant about getting the Word of God in me. And those treasured few minutes of time between tasks became an opportunity to do just that!

One day I noticed that Elwood was struggling with his workload. Being an older gentleman and having spent years of his life doing manual labor on the dairy farm, his body was simply tuckered out. I decided to ask Scott, my foreman, if I could utilize my waiting time to help Elwood with his part of the job so that we could all move faster and get more pipe laid in a day. Scott told me that I could help Elwood if I wanted to, but I certainly wasn't obligated to do that. I was so happy to help him. I considered it an honor to serve Jesus by serving him. Elwood, on the other hand, didn't appreciate my help at first. In fact he screamed at me and cussed me out. You see, he thought that my helping him with his part would cause the boss to consider getting rid of him and hiring someone else who could move faster. He thought my help would just make him look bad, and he was scared to lose his job. However, something entirely different began to happen. My decision to help Elwood set a precedent among all the guys at work. Soon everyone was helping Elwood and helping each other, and we began to function as a unified team, like a well-oiled machine.

> But if you love those who love you, what credit is that to you? For even sinners love those who love them.
>
> —LUKE 6:32

> By this all men will know that you are My disciples, if you have love for one another.
>
> —JOHN 13:35, NASB

After being at the job for some time, Elwood and Tony started opening up to me because I had been living out what I said I believed. In fact Tony told us our group was producing more than the other pipe crew in the company. I wasn't playing! When it was time to work, I did it because I worked as unto the Lord. I didn't cry to Dan or complain or try to work somewhere else. In the days when Jesus walked the earth, there was a reason so many sinners, liars, thieves, and prostitutes flocked to Him. They had to be around Jesus! However, notice that these days people are not banging down the doors to get into church.

Now, I had been praying for people on the job and not seeing anything happen, but I just kept praying. Tony saw this, and he said, "You really believe what you're talking about."

I said, "Yes!"

He said, "And you're always reading your Bible."

I said "Yes!"

Do you know that less than half of evangelical Christians read the Word of God every day?[1] Imagine if one hundred thousand soldiers went into battle, but less than half of them went in locked and loaded. I told Tony, "I have to get the Word in me because it's alive."

He said, "Yeah, but I've tried to read it, and I don't understand it."

I replied, "Me too, man, but I've found that the Holy Spirit helps me."

See, Tony had been a witness to my conduct. The words I shared with him were carrying weight because my life was honorable. He had been a hoe operator for seventeen years and had never seen someone lay pipe like me. He knew I had no prior pipe-laying experience, so he knew there was something supernatural going on. He could see that my life was different because of God. Imagine yourself being able to do such an amazing job for the people you work for that they give credit to God for you! It can't go unnoticed because it's not normal. God has done it in my life, and He can do it in yours. We have to get the spirit of ugly off of the bride of Christ.

The Holy Spirit wants to use the church as a beautiful example of Jesus.

Two months into the job, things were going amazingly well with our team and our progress. Early one morning we got to a jobsite to prep the ground and get everything ready for the excavators. The ground was frozen to the point that it was a solid sheet of ice. For the first time in my life I stopped to take notice of the sunrise that was then creating a solid beam of light across the ice to the horizon. It was the most beautiful view I had ever seen, and my eyes began to tear up. I was so taken by the sight of it, I didn't notice Elwood walk up behind me until I heard him say, "God did that." Then he turned and walked away. I realized in that moment that God was getting to his heart. I cried tears of gratitude. It was such a special moment.

Something at work came up, and I got transferred to another crew. Later I saw Elwood at a Christmas party for the company. He came and sat by me and my wife, and he said, "Todd, I really wish you were back." Man, that blessed my heart! This guy, who at first hated me because I was a Christian, was now sitting there telling me he missed me. And about six months after I was transferred, Tony called me up one day and asked me to come to his wedding. My wife and I went to the wedding. Then at the reception he asked if I would be willing to make a speech. I was thrilled! See, if I had cried to God to get me out of my job, I would not have been able to make this kind of an impact. I realized from the beginning that I was supposed to be a light shining in the darkness, and my workplace was dark.

Scott saw me at the wedding reception and said, "Todd, I just want you to know I have tried to do everything I can to get you back on our crew, but it didn't go through. I really miss you, man." I told him I loved him, and he said, "I love you too." Think about it. That was a complete turnaround from his original, "Shut up! Get away from me."

Do you have any idea how much weight you have? Everywhere you go, you're a representation of Jesus. Everywhere you go, you impact the people around you, one way or the other. If people can't see Christ in you, they do not want what you have. You need to understand that you have favor with God.

> For You, O LORD, will bless the righteous; with favor
> You will surround him as with a shield.
>
> —PSALM 5:12

You are a steward of God's grace and favor. When you speak an encouraging word, you are speaking life into that person. You are essentially saying, "God, I thank You that I have favor with You, and I am asking You to bestow favor on this person." God will grant favor on others because of the words that you speak. Jesus said His words are spirit and life.

> It is the Spirit who gives life; the flesh profits nothing.
> The words that I speak to you are spirit, and they are life.
>
> —JOHN 6:63

You are a steward of grace to those around you, so speak life! And there's another side of that coin: when you choose to criticize, complain, or gossip—which is the language of hell—then you are choosing to use the tongue God gave you to willingly speak death over someone. You shouldn't do that. You must speak life, love, encouragement, truth, forgiveness, healing, and grace—the full gospel!

At the end of my time at the pipe-laying company, I started to see people getting healed. It didn't start out that way when I first got there. I prayed for people and prayed and prayed, and nothing seemed to be happening. But then people started getting healed! God told me, "Todd, if you can share with the people what I have shared with you and the revelation I have given you and put in your heart, then they will step in at your ceiling and not have to go through the plowing process because you have already plowed." As of this writing, I have watched this word come to fruition, and it's still bearing fruit in my life!

Chapter 8

Healing Is Real

In the last chapter I mentioned there was a point towards the end of my time at the pipe-laying company when I began to see people I prayed for get healed. I want to share with you the background story about this particular change in my life as a full-gospel-believing Christian. You see, so many Christians have not tapped into the power of God to heal sickness and disease, even though we see healing miracles all over the Bible. Healing people was common practice in the everyday lives of Jesus and His disciples.

News flash: healing people is *still* the common practice in the everyday lives of Jesus and His disciples!

He never stopped healing, and neither should we! We know He said we could do it and would do it, but for some reason this particular commission has largely remained unmet in the lives of many Christians because we have not fully understood or believed what Jesus clearly stated. He said, "They will lay hands on the sick, and they will recover."

And these signs will follow those who believe: In My name they will cast out demons; they will speak with new tongues; they will take up serpents; and if they drink anything deadly, it will by no means hurt them; they will lay hands on the sick, and they will recover.

—Mark 16:17–18

It is way past time that all believers access the power of God to heal the sick! The Bible says the same Spirit who raised Jesus from the dead lives in you. That's unfathomable power! The power of God to heal sickness and disease has been given to you for you to be His hands and feet on the earth.

But if the Spirit of Him who raised Jesus from the dead dwells in you, He who raised Christ Jesus from the dead will also give life to your mortal bodies through His Spirit who dwells in you.

—Romans 8:11, nasb

Now to Him who is able to do far more abundantly beyond all that we ask or think, according to the power that works within us, to Him be the glory in the church and in Christ Jesus to all generations forever and ever. Amen.

—Ephesians 3:20–21, nasb

For our gospel did not come to you in word only, but also in power and in the Holy Spirit and with full conviction; just as you know what kind of men we proved to be among you for your sake.

—1 Thessalonians 1:5, nasb

One day I went to a healing service that my mentor, Dan Mohler, was leading. A man and his wife were there because they had heard from their neighbor that God had healed her knee in one of the meetings. They were highly skeptical but decided to come to the meeting as a last resort. You see, the husband had leukemia, and there were only fifty cases of this particular strain of leukemia in the world. The other forty-nine cases had ended in death. The man and his wife came forward and explained to Dan that they were out of medical options at that point; the husband was going to hospice and was expected to die soon. They went on to say that they had been raised in the church and taught their whole lives that healing and miracles were not for today, that healing ended with the disciples. Then the wife said to Dan, "We want to know, because of us not believing anything you shared today, is that going to matter when you pray for my husband?"

I was right beside Dan just listening intently. Dan looked at them and said, "Absolutely not. Let me pray for you." Then he prayed for him.

The man didn't fall down under the power of God or anything—in fact after the prayer he said, "Is that it?"

Dan said, "That's it." Then Dan gave them his number.

I immediately thought of the time Dan gave me his number. So I told them, "You should hold on to that number!"

They took the number and turned around and left. A few days later the man went back to the doctor, and the leukemia was completely gone! I was there when they shared the testimony. I thought, "OH. MY. GOSH! You're kidding me! Man, I'm going to start praying for everybody!" I knew from that point forward, healing was going to be a part of my Christian walk. The night that the healing testimony came in, Dan was preaching on the same verses in Mark 16 that I just referenced: "These signs will follow those who believe . . . they will lay hands on the sick, and they will recover" (vv. 17–18).

After the service I asked Dan, "If God heals in the church, then why wouldn't He heal people outside of the church?"

He replied, "Well, He would!"

I said, "Well then, that's it! I'm going to pray for everybody then!"

My wife and my daughter went to Walmart with me, and I decided to start praying for people in there. I had never seen people praying for other people in public, but I knew God is the same in and out of church. So why wouldn't He heal people out in the world? Plus I am a believer, and since I am a believer, it's going to happen!

So my daughter and I walked over to this elderly lady in a walker and asked if we could pray for her. She said, "In here?"

I said, "Yes ma'am. The worst that could happen is nothing. We have nothing to lose!" It's not hard to lose nothing. She agreed, and we prayed for her.

Afterwards she said, "Well, thanks for trying," and she walked away.

My daughter, who hadn't been in any of the healing meetings at church, didn't know what was going on and asked me, "Daddy, why are we doing this?"

I said, "Because we are believers, honey. This is what we do." Then we went around and prayed for another person and another one and another one. Nothing happened the whole time. We prayed for ten people that night, and nothing happened.

I couldn't find my wife and figured she was probably in the car, as it had been an hour and a half. We got out to the car, and she was furious! "What do you think you're doing? You are not a pastor!" She didn't understand. She hammered me the whole way home. I didn't get mad at her. I just went to my room when I got home, and I prayed for her. Then I came out of the bedroom to talk to her, but she wasn't having it. She was so angry and told me to never do that again in public, but I couldn't stop praying for people.

I made a commitment to pray for at least nine people every day. Sometimes it was twelve, but the average ended up being around ten people. The next time we were out in public together, I started praying for people. My wife said, "I told you never again!"

I said, "Honey, you just don't understand." When we got home, I went back to my bedroom, sought Jesus, and kept praying for her.

This went on week after week. She wouldn't go in public with me anymore except on Sunday. She would only go to church with me because the elders at the church wouldn't allow me to pray for anybody at the church. When I went to class on Saturdays at the church,

I would tell them that I had been praying for people. They would say, "Todd, you can't just pray for people. Who is your covering? Who gave you the authority to just go around praying for everybody?"

I said, "Well, Jesus did. I'm a believer. I understand I'm not allowed to pray for anyone in here because you told me that I can't, but I need to keep praying for people out there."

They insisted I needed a spiritual father, someone to mentor me, so I went to Dan. I said, "Dan, you're my spiritual father."

He said, "Todd, it sounds right, what you're saying, and I understand why you're saying it—because people are telling you that you need a spiritual father. Todd, you can glean from me and learn from me, but if God doesn't become your Father all the time, then someday you'll call me, and I won't be there, and you'll feel like you're an orphan." Dan was saying that I can't just rely on him to be my spiritual father. He was saying that I need to make God my Father first and foremost so that I know that I'm a son. It's OK to be a spiritual father, but a spiritual father should always push you into the arms of your heavenly Father because an earthly father can't be there for you all the time the way God is.

> Do not call anyone on earth your father; for One is your Father, He who is in heaven.
>
> —Matthew 23:9

"You're my mentor then, because they said I need a mentor."

"Todd, it sounds right, what you're saying, and I understand, and I can teach you and help you, and you can glean from me. But if the Holy Spirit doesn't become your teacher, doesn't become your mentor, then you will always be needing someone else to teach you, instead of the teacher who will teach you internally when something comes your way—to show you whether it's truth or not. He is the Spirit of truth. So the Father God is your Father, and the Holy Spirit is your spiritual mentor. This doesn't mean you're in rebellion; it means you're in relationship."

"Well then, who are you?"

"I'm your friend."

"You're like the best friend ever!"

He replied, "The Holy Spirit is your best friend."

Dan did everything he could to push me into relationship with Jesus. He did nothing to draw me to him and away from my heavenly Father. He didn't want me to be codependent on him; he always directed me into the arms of God.

For three months I had been praying for about seventy people a week, and no one I prayed for had received healing. I didn't see people get out of wheelchairs. I didn't see any knees get healed—not a pinky, not a toe, not even a headache. The elders told me, "Well, Todd, it's obviously not your gift."

Others said, "Obviously the reason God is not answering your prayers is because your wife isn't on the same page."

But I knew in my heart that I wasn't in rebellion. I wasn't trying to be some lone ranger. I just wanted to believe that the Bible was the unadulterated, complete Word of God and that His Word was going to be higher than what I wasn't seeing happen. If I came across a situation that didn't line up with it, it wasn't because God didn't want it to happen, because His Word is true regardless. I never allowed what I didn't see to influence what I needed to see—and that's what kept me going. Jesus is the will of God, and if Jesus touched someone, the person was healed. So that's my goal!

I never complained to God about not answering my prayers for my wife. I spent thirty-four years of my life denying Jesus, despising Him, and rejecting Him. If Jesus waited thirty-four years for me because I was the joy set before Him, then my wife was worth waiting for.

When I came out of Teen Challenge, I sought the Lord, and He said, "I'm stamping Matthew 6:33 on your forehead, and you're going to live by it and see it every day." That verse says:

> But seek first the kingdom of God and His righteous-
> ness, and all these things shall be added to you.
>
> —MATTHEW 6:33

Well, my wife was part of that "added" thing, but I had to seek first the reality of His kingdom and righteousness and what that means—because everything else hinges on it. The keys to the whole kingdom are seeking Him first and His righteousness. The kingdom is not meat or drink, but it is righteousness, peace, and joy in the Holy Spirit!

For the kingdom of God is not eating and drinking, but righteousness and peace and joy in the Holy Spirit.

—Romans 14:17, NASB

That's the kingdom, and I have to seek it to understand it. And if it's so simple that Jesus said that unless you become like a child, you'll never get it, then maybe we have become too smart in thinking about all these other things and reading a thousand books to understand. All we really need to do is this one thing! This is what I have sought since the beginning.

When I look at the life of Jesus, I see that every time He laid hands on the sick, they recovered! He's my model! Now Jesus said He could do nothing of Himself but only what He saw the Father doing.

Then Jesus answered and said to them, "Most assuredly, I say to you, the Son can do nothing of Himself, but what He sees the Father do; for whatever He does, the Son also does in like manner."

—John 5:19

Whatever the Father did, the Son did in like manner. It was the Holy Spirit in and upon Jesus who healed the sick. This is the same power of God unto salvation! It's the righteousness of God, and He made His home inside of us so that we could represent Him on this earth and everywhere we go. Everywhere we go, we can have Him flow through us like a river. Rivers aren't scared. We can't have the fear of man. Do you know that to know the love of God is to be filled with the fullness of God?

> ... to know the love of Christ which passes knowledge; that you may be filled with all the fullness of God.
>
> —Ephesians 3:19

Everything hinges on the love of God. If I live my life to receive honor from other people, the love of God is not in me. We grow up in the world, trying to do things to impress people so that we can get a thank-you from them, but when we come to Christ, we live to be a thank-you to God, regardless of how people treat us.

If we hunger and thirst for righteousness, we will be filled.

> Blessed are those who hunger and thirst for righteousness, for they shall be filled.
>
> —Matthew 5:6

At the same time, you're also blessed when you are persecuted for what you hunger and thirst for.

> Blessed are those who are persecuted for righteousness' sake, for theirs is the kingdom of heaven.
>
> —Matthew 5:10

Earnestly desire the spiritual gifts, but without a hunger and thirst for righteousness, you will walk in gifting at the cost of identity, which means you are in trouble. What are you living for? Is it to receive praise from man? If so, you'll die in that place.

> Pursue love, and desire spiritual gifts, but especially that you may prophesy.
>
> −1 CORINTHIANS 14:1

After Jesus rose from the dead, He appeared to the disciples in the place where they were hiding because of fear of the Jews. He immediately said, "Peace be with you." Then He breathed on them and said, "Receive the Holy Spirit."

> Then, the same day at evening, being the first day of the week, when the doors were shut where the disciples were assembled, for fear of the Jews, Jesus came and stood in the midst, and said to them, "Peace be with you." When He had said this, He showed them His hands and His side. Then the disciples were glad when they saw the Lord.
>
> So Jesus said to them again, "Peace to you! As the Father has sent Me, I also send you." And when He had said this, He breathed on them, and said to them, "Receive the Holy Spirit. If you forgive the sins of any, they are forgiven them; if you retain the sins of any, they are retained."
>
> −JOHN 20:19−23

When Jesus breathed on the disciples and they received the Holy Spirit, it was their born-again experience.

It was God breathing back into dirt–breathing back into man again and restoring creation. That's amazing, but that wasn't all . . . because then Jesus told them to wait to be endued with power. Not like a little power. Not like a firecracker or dynamite. This power is greater than any nuclear weapon on the planet. This power is the greatest power in existence–God Himself. He was telling them that they were about to be clothed in the power of God Himself!

> When the Day of Pentecost had fully come, they were all with one accord in one place. And suddenly there came a sound from heaven, as of a rushing mighty wind, and it filled the whole house where they were sitting. Then there appeared to them divided tongues, as of fire, and one sat upon each of them. And they were all filled with the Holy Spirit and began to speak with other tongues, as the Spirit gave them utterance.
>
> —Acts 2:1-4

Jesus had told them to wait and pray in Jerusalem, so they were all in one place. They were all in unity, waiting for the Holy Spirit to come. They didn't know what it was going to look like; they just knew it was coming because Jesus said so. John the Baptist also spoke of the coming of Jesus, the Holy Spirit, and a baptism of fire.

> As for me, I baptize you with water for repentance, but He who is coming after me is mightier than I, and I am

not fit to remove His sandals; He will baptize you with
the Holy Spirit and fire.

—MATTHEW 3:11, NASB

There is so much more available to the believer than
salvation alone. Yes, Jesus wants you born again—but He
doesn't want you to stop there! He wants to baptize you
in the Holy Spirit and fire! He wants you to walk in the
fullness of the gospel, which is a gospel of power!

For our gospel did not come to you in word only, but
also in power and in the Holy Spirit and with full conviction; just as you know what kind of men we proved
to be among you for your sake.

—1 THESSALONIANS 1:5, NASB

For the kingdom of God does not consist in words
but in power.

—1 CORINTHIANS 4:20, NASB

I had been praying for all of these people, and I had
not seen one of them receive their healing. It was still
exciting for me to step past fear, but I longed to see the
Word of God made manifest with power. I was missing
something that I didn't know I needed. I was missing the
baptism of the Holy Spirit and fire!

One day there was a healing conference near my
home at the time, in Harrisburg, PA. Bill Johnson and
Randy Clark were some of the speakers there. I showed
up to the conference so excited to learn more about
healing! During my prayer time leading up to the

meeting, I kept thinking about Matthew 3:11. "He will baptize you with the Holy Spirit and fire." I couldn't get that phrase out of my head! I prayed and asked the Lord, "What is this? I want this! I feel like this is missing in my life!" I began to cry out to the Lord for a baptism of the Holy Spirit and fire.

When it was Randy Clark's turn to preach at the conference, I started to feel heat course through my body while he was talking. Suddenly Randy pointed me out in the crowd of 1,600 people and said, "Son, you've been praying for the Holy Ghost and fire, haven't you?" Then he said, "Stand up."

When I stood from my seat, this intense power that felt like electricity and fire came and knocked me to the floor. I began to scream. I was afraid because I did not know that I was experiencing what I had prayed for. You see, this wasn't a slight touch from Jesus. It wasn't goose bumps. It was a complete immersion in the Holy Spirit that saturated me to the core, and it physically hurt! I was on the floor screaming, "Help!" But I could barely talk because it felt like an elephant was standing on me.

You know, some Christians say things such as, "Well, I don't like when people move and shake and fall to the floor in church."

My response is, "Do you believe in God? How big is God? He's infinitely big! And when something infinitely big touches something this small, there is bound to be some kind of reaction!"

Some people say, "I'm not really comfortable with that." It's because they need the Comforter! People are so afraid of looking like fools, but how are they ever going to talk about Jesus with the world if they are afraid of looking like fools?

What if you're afraid to talk to your neighbor about Jesus because the last time you shared the gospel with someone, you got shut down? Are you going to let the fear of that happening again keep you clammed up? One day your neighbor is going to stand at the throne of judgment. How would it feel to be standing in the sheep line with your neighbor in the goat line, screaming, "Why didn't you tell me?" Then your neighbor will go to eternal condemnation because of your little fear on this planet. That won't be me! Decide that won't be you either. Let's not go out that way. Life is short–leave a legacy.

So there I was on the floor of the church, wailing and yelling, "Help!" as intense heat and power coursed through my body.

Randy said, "He won't die. More Lord!" And it kept coming–it was as if electricity was coursing through my body, and then it intensified! I was holding on to the chair for dear life! When it finally subsided, my muscles ached, my joints ached, and I was worn out. Later I was out in the lobby, and Randy Clark saw me and came towards me.

I said, "Please don't touch me."

He said, "What's your name, son?

"Todd."

"What do you do?"

I shared a little, but I couldn't get all the words out. I was still incapacitated.

"You were praying for this to happen."

"Yeah, but I didn't know it was going to be like this!"

"Everything changes from this point! This is the most beautiful encounter! Up until this day I have never seen this happen without me laying hands on someone."

It was a sovereign move of God because of the hunger in my heart. I need to see everyone get out of every wheelchair. I need to see every blind eye open. I need to see the spirit of holiness touch the bride of Christ. I need to see Christians understand that Jesus isn't coming back for a wrinkled bride—He is coming back for a spotless bride. I need to see the church understand that she is called to a holiness we are not yet walking in. We are called to be holy as He is holy.

> You shall be holy, for I the LORD your God am holy.
>
> —LEVITICUS 19:2

The bride of Christ is called to have a pure heart. The lack of purity in the bride is in equal proportion to the condemnation the bride carries. The lack of purity someone walks in is in equal proportion to the person's guilty conscience because it hasn't been washed by the blood of Jesus. The bride has to get her heart right because Jesus is coming back for a pure church He can dwell in.

You have to have communion with the Holy Ghost. You have to cultivate your relationship with God. You cannot have communion if you have no union, and you cannot have union if you have sin separating you from Him. You need Him. You need the baptism of the Holy Spirit.

After the meeting with Randy Clark I was filled with the Holy Spirit. By the following week the evidence of that baptism began to manifest. During the previous three and a half months I had prayed for an average of seventy people a week, and I did not see a single person get healed. That changed after I received the baptism of the Holy Spirit and fire. Within a week of that encounter, the Holy Spirit gave me my first word of knowledge. I didn't even know what a word of knowledge was at that time, but I got one for a Catholic man about a problem with two disks in his back and sciatic nerve damage down his right leg. When I asked him if this was the problem, he said, "Yes!"

I was amazed and said, "I'm a Christian!"

"I'm Catholic."

"Cool, look right here."

I showed him Mark 16:17–18: "These signs will follow those who believe . . . " Then, understanding he was Catholic, I told him that Mary gave birth to Jesus, and Jesus is His Savior.

He agreed, "Yes!"

"At the wedding in Cana the last thing that Mary said was, 'Do whatever Jesus tells you!'"

"All right. Let's do it. What do we do?"

I prayed for him, and he was healed! He exclaimed, "You have a power!"

I said, "No, it's Jesus! It's the Holy Spirit! He lives in me!" We were both so excited! I blessed him and told him God loves him. Then I went to call my wife to tell her. Before I could even get to the end of the testimony to tell her he was healed, she hung up on me.

Then I called Dan and told him. He was so proud of me for not giving up.

When I got home from work that day, I tried again to tell Jackie, but she just told me I was crazy. I said, "I know!" After that there was another healing that week. The next week there were three, then four—so I began praying for even more people because I was seeing more people get healed. See, I decided to focus on what God was doing instead of what He was not doing. After about six months of seeing people get healed, it would take me an hour and a half every day just to write out all of the testimonies! Finally the Lord told me I didn't have to write them down anymore as He had logged them in my heart. To this day, when I remember them, I can see them played out like a video in my mind's eye.

Meanwhile I continued to get persecuted by my wife. Jackie knew I was different because there wasn't any sin in my life. My language had changed, my conduct had changed, and my attitude had changed. There wasn't anything my wife could point a finger at except that everywhere I went, I prayed for people to be healed. That's an amazing thing to suffer for! If I suffer for doing good, it's commendable before God, but if I suffer for doing bad, what profit is that? If I suffer as an evildoer for doing bad, it's no good at all—it's actually damages the gospel. If I suffer for doing good because I believe the gospel, and I walk it out, then the only thing I am being persecuted for is for righteousness' sake. This is commendable before the Lord, and great is my reward. Never drop this standard!

For this finds favor, if for the sake of conscience toward God a person bears up under sorrows when suffering unjustly. For what credit is there if, when you sin and are harshly treated, you endure it with patience? But if when you do what is right and suffer for it you patiently endure it, this finds favor with God.

–1 PETER 2:19–20, NASB

Now, I remember there was one night when Jackie said she wanted to go out to eat with me, but she said, "You will not pray for anybody!" When we arrived at the restaurant, God began speaking to me about some people there, sitting at a table near ours—a very young grandma, a teenage mom, and the mom's two-year old daughter. All three generations were there, having dinner. God showed me a picture of the grandmother's husband, the young mom's stepdad. He showed me that this man had molested her and told her that God wanted it to happen. He used the name of Jesus to sexually abuse his stepdaughter. The Lord told me to tell this young mom that this was very wrong and it was not of Him. He would never have someone do that to her. And He wanted me to tell her He loves her very much. I told my wife what I had heard from the Lord and that I had to say something because this situation in the mom's past was separating her from the Lord.

My wife said, "You better not!" We already had our food ordered. She said, "We will eat, and we will leave, and we will leave quickly! You will not go pray for her!" So I went to the bathroom, and I told the Lord that I didn't know what to say or what to do with this. This was the first time Jackie had been willing to go anywhere in public with me in months. What was I going to do? It just so happened that we got up the exact same time these women did. My wife said, "Oh my God," and she ran out of the door and went to the car.

I held the door open for everyone, and as the woman passed by me, I said, "Excuse me, ma'am. I saw what your stepdad did."

She said, "What?"

I said, "I saw what he did. He claimed to be a Christian, but that is not what Christians would do. And I'm telling you right now that God knows you, and He loves you, and I'm sorry that this happened. God would never, ever, ever do those things to you."

She began to cry and said, "You have no idea."

"I do. It's horrible. But Jesus would never do that to you. He loves you."

She looked at me with tears streaming down her face and said, "I just want to thank you. I don't even know what to say."

"Just know that God loves you, and I repent on behalf of your stepfather. I'm so sorry he did that to you. Please don't turn your back on God."

"OK. Thank you so much!"

When I got to our car, my wife was livid! She swore she would never go out in public with me again. But I knew I had heard from the Lord and obeyed Him. I knew that young woman needed to know God's true heart towards her.

Several months went by, and I continued to pray for people everywhere I went. My daughter and I would go to the grocery store to buy food and end up staying there for long periods of time because we were praying for people. Jackie was fed up with our trips taking so long, so she decided to go with my daughter and me to the store to make things move faster. She said, "OK. Here is what is going to happen: I am going to go to the grocery store with you. You will not see me there. You will go this way, and I will go that way. You will get these things, and I will get those things. You have a debit card, and I have a debit card. I will meet you in the car when we're done. Do *not* talk to me there!"

My daughter and I prayed together for my wife. I told Destiny, "Mommy isn't hurting Daddy. Mommy is just hurting inside, and we need to pray for her, that she would know who she is in Jesus." I never spoke badly about Jackie to my daughter because Jackie was her mom, and God had given her to me as a wife–as a gift! I've never lost focus of my wife being my best friend. No matter how angry she got, she was still my girl. She'll always be my girl. She's the woman God gave me. See, I never prayed for my wife so that my life would get easier, because that is not prayer. That's selfishness. That would be praying for her *for me*, not praying for her *for her*. Instead I prayed for God to touch her so that she would see who she was as a daughter of God. I thanked God for her and the blessing that she was.

That day my daughter said to me, "Mommy is going to the store with us. We had better not pray for anybody."

I said, "Well, Mommy is going to be way over there on the other side of the store." So we went in the store, and two aisles down I saw a lady in a scooter. We ran up to her and said, "Hey, may we pray for you?"

The lady said, "That's OK. I don't want prayer. Richard Roberts prays for me every night when he asks those who need healing to stretch their hands towards the screen."

I said, "Well, we are members of the body of Christ too! Can we pray too?"

She answered, "No."

So I began trying to think of a way to get this lady to let me pray for her. I looked at her granddaughter and said, "Hey, would you like your grandma to be able to play with you?"

"Yeah," she said. She turned to her grandma. "Grandma, let him pray for you!"

The lady said, "I cannot believe that you would stoop to this place." What she was essentially saying was, "How dare you get my granddaughter's hopes up?"

See, we teach people not to get their hopes up, but faith says, "Get your hopes up!" Way up!

> Now faith is the substance of things hoped for, the evidence of things not seen.
>
> —HEBREWS 11:1

So the lady finally agreed, and said, "Fine! Hurry up!" Some people would argue that she needed to deal with her unforgiveness before God could heal her. But we need to remember that it is the goodness of the Lord that draws people to repentance.

Or do you despise the riches of His goodness, forbearance, and longsuffering, not knowing that the goodness of God leads you to repentance?

—ROMANS 2:4

Sometimes we try to deal with people's unforgiveness before they see the goodness of God, but it's a lot easier the other way around. Once people see how good He is, they just can't hold on to unforgiveness any longer—because He is just that awesome!

The lady let us pray, and I asked her if she was feeling anything.

She replied, "No. Honey, I have had four back surgeries, and my spine is fused in this seated position. For twenty-seven years I have not been able to stand up straight, and I've been on chronic pain medication that I can't even afford."

I asked if she could just try to move or stand. She tried, but she started to sweat from the pain. So we prayed again. This time all three of us, including her granddaughter, laid our hands on her and commanded her back to be healed in the name of Jesus. All of a sudden we heard a loud pop. Her eyes bugged out in shock. Her back popped right there in the store. I had never heard anything like it before.

She began to stand, and her granddaughter started crying tears of joy. She said, "Grandma, run!"

The lady said, "Run? I can hardly walk!"

"Come on, Grandma," she said, "run!" They ran down the aisle and then ran back, and she was out of breath. She hadn't even stood up straight in 27 years, and she was now able to run.

Right then my wife walked in our aisle. My daughter immediately ran and hid behind me. "Oh no, Daddy. What are we going to do?" There was nowhere to hide. She said, "Mommy is really, really mad."

The grandma asked what was wrong, and I explained that my wife just didn't understand why I pray for people. I said, "Do you think you could talk to her and tell her what just happened?"

The grandma said, "Sure I will!" She went over to Jackie to tell her what had happened. I prayed under my breath. The lady turned and lifted up her shirt to show Jackie the scar where they had previously fused her spine. Then she bent over and touched the floor. Jackie began to cry. The grandma and Jackie embraced each other, and I began to cry. It was so powerful. We paid for our groceries and left the store. No one said a word the entire drive home.

When we got home, I carried in all the groceries and put everything away. Then I went back in my bedroom and thanked God for the endurance to be able to witness my wife discover her created value. I prayed for the elders at my church and every member of my family—that they would all come to know their created value too. And I thanked God for enabling me to see with the eyes of the Lord.

I came out of the room after about an hour and a half of praying and crying. My wife was on the couch, crying. I said, "Are you OK?"

She said, "No, God spoke to me."

I said, "What did He say?"

She said, "He said, 'I've given you a new husband, a new man, one that you never knew existed. He believes Me. Now why won't you?'"

I said, "Oh my gosh. What are you going to do?"

She said, "From this day forward I will never stand in the way of God again."

See, what I had been telling her all along was great, but when God told her, it meant everything. Have faith in the seed you're sowing out there in the world today. Have faith in the seed you're sowing in and amongst your family, even if they tell you everything opposite to what you're believing for. Don't faint, and don't grow weary in doing good, because in due season you will reap if you faint not, no matter what.

> And let us not grow weary while doing good, for in due season we shall reap if we do not lose heart.
>
> —GALATIANS 6:9

My wife calls that season of life "labor" because it was nine months before her unbelief broke. It was a season of labor pains that gave birth to something amazing. Now together we get to display God's love to the world around us. There's no other person I'd rather crush hell with. Jackie is my best friend.

Don't wait for a word of knowledge to come before you're willing to minister to those around you. Let me ask you something: Why would God give words of knowledge to people who aren't willing to act on what they already know? Act on what you already know. Give what you already have, and you'll be given more. If you're faithful with the little that you have, you will be given much more.

He who is faithful in a very little thing is faithful also in much; and he who is unrighteous in a very little thing is unrighteous also in much.

—LUKE 16:10, NASB

Whatever you do in word or deed, do all in the name of the Lord Jesus, giving thanks through Him to God the Father.

—COLOSSIANS 3:17, NASB

Everything you do, do as unto the Lord. We must be heavenly minded. You see, to be truly heavenly minded means that you are full of love for God and love for people, and so scripturally saturated that the Word of God has completely renewed your mind. Heaven is seeking after people to fill it, so this should be your agenda too. If you're the only one who knows you're a Christian at your workplace, then something is wrong. Don't try to get out of your workplace to get into ministry. Realize your workplace is your mission field. Everywhere you go, you're called to minister. If you're not even willing to talk to the people who are around you on a daily basis, what makes you think God wants to put you in a place of ministry where you'll be the head of a bunch of people? Be willing to sow seeds of the kingdom right where you're at, and watch what God does through that. He'll take what you have and multiply it. It's so simple. Be who He created you to be in right standing with Him, in relationship with Him, and give out of that place—right here, right now, right where you are in life!

Chapter 9

True Identity

M y goal is to disable the enemy's plans to stop people from sharing their faith. The devil is petrified that you might dare to share your faith wherever you go. You know, it's very hard to share your faith and the gospel if you really don't believe in it. It's very hard to share your faith with confidence if you really don't believe in what you're sharing. Outside of the gospel and outside of the Word of God, all we have is human wisdom–the wisdom of man. And the Bible shows us that the wisdom of man is in opposition to the wisdom of God.

Who among you is wise and understanding? Let him show by his good behavior his deeds in the gentleness of wisdom. But if you have bitter jealousy and selfish ambition in your heart, do not be arrogant and so lie against the truth. This wisdom is not that which comes down from above, but is earthly, natural, demonic. For where jealousy and selfish ambition exist, there is disorder and every evil thing. But the wisdom from above is first pure, then peaceable, gentle, reasonable, full of mercy and good fruits, unwavering, without hypocrisy. And the seed whose fruit is righteousness is sown in peace by those who make peace.

—JAMES 3:13–18, NASB

Every evil thing comes from the wisdom of man. We have all been trained in the wisdom of man by the world—selfish ambition, arrogance, looking out for number one, being first, and doing whatever you have to do to get to the top, even if it's at someone else's expense. Even if you grew up in church, you were still trained with that wisdom by the influence of the world around you. It's the way that seems right to a man, but it ends in destruction.

There is a way that seems right to a man, but its end is the way of death.

—PROVERBS 14:12

The wisdom of God is completely opposite. In His kingdom the first will be last. The wisdom of God is pure, peaceful, gentle, reasonable, full of mercy and good fruits, unwavering, and without hypocrisy. This is the wisdom that we're seeking. The majority of people are going down the broad path after the wisdom of this age, but Jesus is the narrow way, and few go down it.

> Enter through the narrow gate; for the gate is wide and the way is broad that leads to destruction, and there are many who enter through it. For the gate is small and the way is narrow that leads to life, and there are few who find it.
>
> —MATTHEW 7:13–14, NASB

Out of all the people who answer the call of God on their lives, few actually find the path that leads to it. It's so simple that you have to become like a child to find it, but because we're so smart and because we're problem fixers, we often miss the answers Jesus has already given us. This gospel is not psychological. Psychology is the way that seems right to a man. Jesus didn't change the gospel to fit our textbooks and our drug-rehabilitation programs and our self-help manuals. You know some people would hear my testimony of being addicted to drugs for over twenty-two years and say, "Well, once an addict, always an addict." Well, I guess . . . if you mean I'm addicted to Jesus! But Jesus crushed every other addiction I had! There is no chain He can't break. Our number one addiction has to be intimacy with the Lord. If we don't go into the secret place to seek Him, then we'll have secrets. But secrets get annihilated when you realize you've been forgiven. The issue occurs when you don't believe you're forgiven. We know the blood of Jesus cleanses us from all sin. He paid the price on the cross to forgive your sin, and He also paid the price to forget your sin. He removes your transgressions as far as the east is from the west.

> As far as the east is from the west, so far has He
> removed our transgressions from us.
>
> —PSALM 103:12, NASB

Do you know when you keep traveling east, you will never end up going west? That is the good news!

A lot of people talk about the time in their lives when they found God. Let me tell you something. You didn't find God—God found you! He might let you think you found Him for a while, but when you open your Bible, you'll know that it was actually Him who found you, because no one comes to the Father unless he's drawn.

> No one can come to Me unless the Father who sent Me
> draws him; and I will raise him up at the last day.
>
> —JOHN 6:44

If the grace that drew you to God is real, then why would God draw you to Him, just to bring a cross that's only good for emotional freedom for one day? The cross isn't good for emotional freedom for just one day—it is good for having a conscience that has been removed of every sin and every stain for a lifetime.

> The wicked flee when no one pursues, but the righ-
> teous are bold as a lion.
>
> —PROVERBS 28:1

The Lion is amazing. He's bold. You don't have to defend Him; you just have to let Him out of the cage. One person in Christ is a majority—but if I don't realize who I am in Christ, then there are a lot of devils I'll be afraid of. Tell me one devil that Jesus was afraid of. I'll wait . . .

When Jesus was presented with a person with demonic possession, He didn't say, "Oh no! What are we going to do?" or "What kind of program can we take him to so he can learn to control these unhealthy behaviors?" or "Oh man! This is really dark and scary stuff—I really don't know if we should even address this. It's too dangerous." Can you imagine Jesus contemplating such things? Of course not! He didn't entertain devils or try to get them to talk. Do you think demons would even tell the truth? I don't believe in speaking to demons to ask them questions or have a conversation. I'm not around to have a conversation with devils. If I come around, they have to get out.

Listen, the righteous are as bold as a lion, and the self-righteous are only bold in arrogance. True righteous boldness comes from the reality of being blameless in the eyes of the Father. It's confidence in who you are in Jesus and His finished work on the cross. What would it look like for you to go through life without any guilt, shame, condemnation, or regret? It would look like the New Testament! You see, in the Old Testament you had to keep all the laws to obtain righteousness, and no one could do it. That's why we needed Jesus our Messiah.

> For whoever shall keep the whole law, and yet stumble in one point, he is guilty of all.
>
> —James 2:10

There was no way anyone could be righteous in his or her own strength. No flesh was justified. It was impossible. God didn't want it that way. People chose it that way. When God came on Mount Sinai, the children of Israel saw it. They told Moses to talk to God for them because they thought if they came near God, they would die. They used Moses as their mediator. But the Old Testament prophesied of a new Mediator who would come to bring about a new covenant and make a way for mankind to obtain righteousness through Him. This is Jesus! And this covenant is the gospel that has set us free from guilt, shame, and the bondage of sin. You can live a life completely resistant to sinning on purpose. For far too long, Christians have promoted the weakness of the flesh. They say, "My spirit is willing, but my flesh is *weak!*" And they put emphasis on the latter part. They amplify the weakness of the flesh instead of the strength of the spirit.

But we are not in an old covenant. There is a false teaching on grace that has infiltrated the church. False grace says, "It's OK. Let's just sin because God understands, and I'm under grace." But then you can't be free from sin! Some people assume we can't even breathe without sinning. This is what happens when people don't understand the reality of the cost that was paid for them. This is what happens to people's thinking when they don't understand the value system of heaven—they start their lives out as new believers under false teachers who teach a doctrine that says they are still guilty and worthless wretches without value, and it sure was nice of Jesus to pity you and die for your little scum of a life. NO! God doesn't think that way of you! God valued you so much that He sent His Son to die as a payment that you were worthy of. The price that heaven paid for you is in equal proportion to the value your Father God placed on you. The Bible says whoever believes in Jesus will not perish but have eternal life. Do you think eternal life starts *only* when you die? Because it doesn't. John 17 shows us that it starts here when we come to know Him!

> For God so loved the world that He gave His only begotten Son, that whoever believes in Him should not perish but have everlasting life.
>
> —JOHN 3:16

> And this is eternal life, that they may know You, the only true God, and Jesus Christ whom You have sent.
>
> —JOHN 17:3

That's eternal life! It's about knowing God—not talking about God but intimately knowing Him. How can you intimately know Him if you're still guilty, ashamed, and condemned every day of your life? You can't. You can't know Him in relationship if you don't understand your value. You can have an intimate relationship with the Father who loves you profusely and gave up everything to get you back because He thought you were worth it. His thoughts for you outnumber the grains of sand on the earth.

> How precious also are Your thoughts to me, O God! How vast is the sum of them! If I should count them, they would outnumber the sand.
>
> —PSALM 139:17–18, NASB

Your Father determines your identity, which is why the pharisaical teachers of today, operating under a false humility and teaching a false doctrine, identify themselves as worthless wretches. It's because they are identifying with their father, the devil. Satan is the rejected one, the guilty one, the shameful one—and all he can produce is more of his own kind.

In all my years as a Christian I have never been rejected by a person. I've been yelled at, spit on, pushed, and shoved, but I have never been rejected, because I don't gain my acceptance from people. I have been accepted by my Father. I am accepted in the Beloved, so I can't be rejected by people—because people can't take away what they never gave me.

> He chose us in Him before the foundation of the world, that we should be holy and without blame before Him in love, having predestined us to adoption as sons by Jesus Christ to Himself, according to the good pleasure of His will, to the praise of the glory of His grace, by which He made us accepted in the Beloved.
>
> —EPHESIANS 1:4–6

If you're living by the applause and praise of men, you can just as easily die by the criticism of men.

> Blessed are those who are persecuted for righteousness' sake, for theirs is the kingdom of heaven.
>
> —MATTHEW 5:10

If you're looking for the praise of men, then when you're persecuted for righteousness' sake, you won't feel blessed; you'll feel cursed. Then you might water down your message and make up a new one that will win you more likes on your social media account, more numbers in church attendance, and more pats on the back for being "relevant." You won't approach subjects that people don't want to hear. You'll create a platform that is all about pleasing people. You'll create a huge movement that looks just like you, and then one day you'll stand before God and have to answer for it all.

You can't afford to put any confidence in your flesh, no matter how shipshape or impressive it may seem. Your flesh is in complete opposition to God, and it cannot produce anything of the Spirit. This ties back into the difference between man's wisdom and the wisdom from above that we discussed earlier. In the Book of Philippians, Paul talked about his personal background as a devout Jew and Pharisee. Paul was a native Israelite from the tribe of Benjamin. He was brought up under a well-known teacher of the Law, and Paul in his own right was considered a scholar who taught according to the exact pattern of the Law. If anyone among men could put confidence in his pedigree and accolades, it was Paul. And yet, when he reflected on all these things, he counted them as of zero value compared to knowing Jesus and understanding what Jesus did for him.

But whatever things were gain to me, those things I have counted as loss for the sake of Christ. More than that, I count all things to be loss in view of the surpassing value of knowing Christ Jesus my Lord, for whom I have suffered the loss of all things, and count them but rubbish so that I may gain Christ, and may be found in Him, not having a righteousness of my own derived from the Law, but that which is through faith in Christ, the righteousness which comes from God on the basis of faith, that I may know Him and the power of His resurrection and the fellowship of His sufferings, being conformed to His death; in order that I may attain to the resurrection from the dead.

Not that I have already obtained it or have already become perfect, but I press on so that I may lay hold of that for which also I was laid hold of by Christ Jesus. Brethren, I do not regard myself as having laid hold of it yet; but one thing I do: forgetting what lies behind and reaching forward to what lies ahead, I press on toward the goal for the prize of the upward call of God in Christ Jesus.

—Philippians 3:7–14, nasb

Paul chose to forget what was behind him and press toward the call of God in His Son, Jesus! To forget something means you stop thinking about it all together. You can't forget something that you keep rehearsing in your mind. And you won't stop rehearsing in your head what you haven't resolved in your heart, once and for all. You need a clean conscience. Your conscience is the very place that sin defiled, and it is the same place Jesus wants to wash clean from every dead work so that you can serve God.

For our proud confidence is this: the testimony of our conscience, that in holiness and godly sincerity, not in fleshly wisdom but in the grace of God, we have conducted ourselves in the world, and especially toward you.

—2 CORINTHIANS 1:12, NASB

Being born again is essential because it unlocks your potential, but it is just the beginning point for every believer. It's where we make contact with the living God. But the first thing the enemy comes to discredit is the power of the blood of Jesus. In other words, I come to the altar and say yes to Jesus, and I am saved, but it doesn't stop there. Jesus didn't tell us to just pray a prayer to get into heaven and that's it. Heaven is our final destination, but the destination point of the Lord is that heaven would get into us through the agency of the Holy Spirit so that we would be equipped to do the works of the ministry. But if you don't know who you are before you do the works of ministry, then you will gain who you are through what you do instead of who God created you to be. In the world people gain who they are by what they do. That is why so many professional athletes end up broke, divorced, depressed, and suicidal after their careers are over. Instead of discovering who they are in Jesus, their entire identities are wrapped up in what they do, and when they can no longer do it, they're utterly lost. This is why it's so imperative that all new born-again believers come to know who God says they are in Christ as a new creation.

You protect this newfound understanding of your identity in Christ by taking captive every thought that goes against it.

. . . casting down arguments and every high thing that exalts itself against the knowledge of God, bringing every thought into captivity to the obedience of Christ.

−2 Corinthians 10:5

You have to know God's Word! If you don't know His Word, then you will not be able to take thoughts captive that go against it. And if you know the Word without the indwelling of the Holy Spirit, then the thoughts can't be taken captive. Maybe the epidemic in the body of Christ is that we don't know what the Bible says. Or maybe it is being trained in religion under a works mentality instead of a sonship mentality. You have to be son conscious, not sin conscious. Religion trains the soul to be sin conscious; relationship trains the soul to be son conscious. When you have relationship with God, you can boldly approach the throne of grace in your time of need. You can't have boldness without righteousness, because if you don't believe you're right with God, then you won't believe God wants to talk to you. And that is twisted thinking.

Let us therefore come boldly to the throne of grace, that we may obtain mercy and find grace to help in time of need.

−Hebrews 4:16

God loves you, and He is looking at you. You can't look back at Him if you don't have confidence in who He says you are, so you must believe what He says about you and realize every person you encounter has that same value to the Father.

The devil doesn't mind if you go to church, and He may not shake when you share your faith, but he would tremble if you could live a day without condemnation. He would hate it! Why? Because the devil is condemned. He's angry, bitter, ashamed, afraid, and in total unforgiveness, and all he can do is try to re-create his mindset in you. As they say, "Misery loves company." He never wants you to understand that you've been given the mind of Christ. He doesn't want you to believe what the Word says and have communion with the Father, because he can't have communion with the Father. He will try to throw every possible problem your way to stop you from being who God created you to be. He never wants you to see who you really are—because once you've discovered that Jesus has set you free and you see who you really are, you'll tell everyone about Him. Think about what it would look like for you to be transformed in your mind to the point you could look in the mirror of His Word with an unveiled face and behold the glory of the Lord. One breath of God in your life can change everything!

> For I am jealous for you with a godly jealousy; for I betrothed you to one husband, so that to Christ I might present you as a pure virgin. But I am afraid that, as the serpent deceived Eve by his craftiness, your minds will be led astray from the simplicity and purity of devotion to Christ.
>
> —2 CORINTHIANS 11:2–3, NASB

Do you realize God looks at you as if you've never sinned? People who don't understand this spend their time worrying and striving and can't enter His rest because they are still operating under the old covenant of works.

For the one who has entered His rest has himself also rested from his works, as God did from His.

—Hebrews 4:10, NASB

I direct these schools called Power & Love. They are like identity training camps. The by-product of this training is incredible results from evangelism outreach. Some would assume that we spend a lot of time discussing how to be an effective witness, but we actually discuss your identity in Christ! When you see who you are, soul winning is the by-product. The miraculous is the result of sonship. If you see the reality of being a son or daughter of God, you'll believe the whole Bible!

If you have a ministry that the blood of Jesus and the finished work of the cross violates, you should not have a ministry. See, some people believe and teach that we can't truly be free, whole, and healed until we get to heaven. That is such a lie! If that's true, death has become your savior—and that's not the gospel. Death is not your savior; Jesus is! The price He paid was for more than just to get you to heaven, or else you would think like hell here until you get there. Jesus made a way for you to be renewed in your spirit and your mind. You need to understand the reality and the power of the blood of Jesus.

Fear is what disables you from sharing your faith, and fear only has a right to you wherever the perfect love of God hasn't gotten to you, because the perfect love of God casts out all fear.

> There is no fear in love; but perfect love casts out fear, because fear involves punishment, and the one who fears is not perfected in love.
>
> −1 JOHN 4:18, NASB

When you see that you are perfectly loved by your Father, there is no one who can scare you. God did not give us a spirit of fear but of power and love and a sound mind.

> For God has not given us a spirit of fear, but of power and of love and of a sound mind.
>
> −2 TIMOTHY 1:7

I know many ministers who carry power, but they are guilty, condemned, and ashamed. I'm not faulting anyone. I know many people who have big ministries, but they constantly battle depression. There have been great pastors doing great works who have put guns in their mouths and taken their own lives. As of this writing, I know of two who committed suicide just this past year. Why? Because righteousness never hit home! When you see that you're right with God, there is no way that you could take your own life. Your life isn't yours. It's been purchased by the blood of Jesus. Depression has no place to land when righteousness is understood. Depression can prevent people from approaching the throne of grace to obtain mercy and find grace to help in time of need. You'll pray because that's the Christian thing to do, but you won't have intimacy because the depression is just too loud. I know because I lived with depression and suicidal thoughts for years. Then I accepted the gospel of Jesus Christ, and God settled those issues once and for all. The gospel took away all barriers between me and my Father. It will do the same for you if you let it. Jesus loves you!

When Jesus was on the cross, all of your sin, all of your failures, all of your faults, all of your junk was nailed to Him on that tree. Jesus Christ, the Son of God, the Lamb that was slain before the foundation of the world, the One we are to behold, became cursed for us so that we would be free from the curse once and for all. That's why when He was hanging on the cross, He said, "It is finished!" See, Jesus didn't pay the price in His own blood to cover over sin but to remove it completely. You need to know how much it cost to see your sin upon that cross, because God cursed sin in the flesh on that tree. That is amazingly good news!

I have lived in freedom for over fifteen years, with an ever-present awareness that my soul is not condemned, not guilty, and not ashamed. When you know that you're washed, when you know that you're clean, and when you know that you're free, you can talk about that purity and freedom with anyone. You can talk about your freedom with such liberty that no one can shut you down. They might resist, but they can't shut it down. They can't because Jesus is King! God forgave you the same way He forgave me. The reason the body of Christ doesn't love well is they don't believe how much they have been forgiven, because they keep revisiting the things they have been forgiven of. They keep revisiting the things the Lord took away. So the reason they can't love much is because they don't realize how much they have been forgiven.

> For this reason I say to you, her sins, which are many, have been forgiven, for she loved much; but he who is forgiven little, loves little.
>
> —Luke 7:47, nasb

Pray this with me:

Lord Jesus, I'm sorry for not believing what Your Word says. I am asking You to fill me with belief— to believe the simple gospel. Thank You that I am no longer a slave to sin. Thank You that I am not a slave to fear. Thank You that I am Your child. Thank You that I am forgiven. Amen.

Right now I encourage you to take a moment, go look at yourself in the mirror, and speak the word of the Lord over yourself. Settle the truth in your heart and mind with the following declarations:

God lives in me!

God wanted me before I wanted Him!

God has forgiven me for everything!

His cross removed every sin and stain forever!

I stand right before God, completely forgiven and free!

I choose to believe His Word today and every day!

Chapter 10

Complete Transformation

P lease don't ever read the Bible and say to yourself, "I already know this." If you get to that place, then you're unteachable and already done. Every day mercy wakes me up, and I kneel before my King and thank Him that it's a new day! I surrender my life to Jesus each day. People tell me that what I am doing with my life will cost me everything. The only thing it will cost me is something I was never created to be in the first place so I can finally become who He says I really am. In other words, the cost is like trading pebbles in for diamonds. The Father didn't create you for you; He created you for Him. He asks you only to give up what you were never created to be so you can finally become who He says you are. Each new day is a new day for you to manifest God, not you. Grace and mercy woke *you* up this morning. The

Bible says he who seeks to save his life will lose it, but he who loses his life for Jesus' sake will find it. You must die so that you can live.

> For whoever wishes to save his life will lose it; but whoever loses his life for My sake will find it.
> —MATTHEW 16:25, NASB

Say to the Lord, "Jesus, here's my life; I want Yours. God, show me who I am, and I will run with You. I will run with You, and I won't grow weary."

> But those who wait on the LORD shall renew their strength; they shall mount up with wings like eagles, they shall run and not be weary, they shall walk and not faint.
> —ISAIAH 40:31

Say, "God, You're amazing! You're all powerful. Your Word is everything to me. Your Word is a lamp unto my feet."

> Your word is a lamp to my feet and a light to my path.
> —PSALM 119:105

Say, "When I look into Your Word, I am looking into Your very face!"

> In the beginning was the Word, and the Word was with God, and the Word was God.
> —JOHN 1:1

Every time I look into the Word of God, I look into the face of God. And the Word is so powerful that He has magnified it above His name.

> I will worship toward Your holy temple, and praise Your name for Your lovingkindness and Your truth; for You have magnified Your word above all Your name.
>
> —Psalm 138:2

If I were to say that I love God with all that is in me, but I don't love His Word, then that statement wouldn't be true because God has magnified His Word above His name. If you say that you love God, but you don't honor the truth of God's Word and its infallibility, then you really don't love God. When I look into the Word of God with the intimacy of the Holy Spirit and ask Him to make it real to me, He breathes on His Word, and it becomes alive to me.

> For the word of God is living and powerful, and sharper than any two-edged sword, piercing even to the division of soul and spirit, and of joints and marrow, and is a discerner of the thoughts and intents of the heart.
>
> —Hebrews 4:12

And I become a brand-new man every day! Every situation that is given to me is given so that I can glorify Him. Every place I go, no matter how dark it is, the light comes in when I step in, because He lives in me. If I go into a dark area, I don't look and say, "Oh gosh, it's really dark in here." It doesn't matter how dark it is. This is the way I live. If I go into a gym to work out, I have dominion because I have come and Jesus lives in me. If I go to a restaurant, on a plane, in an elevator, to the mall, or to the dental office—wherever I go—He goes with me, and we shake the place. People get touched by Jesus everywhere I go. Why? Because He lives in me. My life is a by-product of my relationship with my King. Jesus is Lord! Nothing can separate me from that but me. Nothing works outside of a relationship with Jesus. You have to have an intimate relationship with Him. When you meet with Him, you become one with Him, and you are transformed into His image.

> Now the Lord is the Spirit, and where the Spirit of the Lord is, there is liberty. But we all, with unveiled face, beholding as in a mirror the glory of the Lord, are being transformed into the same image from glory to glory, just as from the Lord, the Spirit.
>
> —2 CORINTHIANS 3:17–18, NASB

Everything will try to compete with your intimacy with Jesus. Time, business, ministry—those things are good, but you must be very careful to not get caught up in all of that stuff and lose your relationship with Jesus. What good does it do if you talk about the Lord with people, but you have no relationship with Him? Unless the Lord builds the house, the people labor in vain.

Unless the LORD builds the house, they labor in vain who build it; unless the LORD guards the city, the watchman keeps awake in vain.

—PSALM 127:1, NASB

I can preach the truth, but outside of the reality of my relationship with God, the truth won't keep me free. I can quote as many scriptures as I want, but the reality is my love relationship with God is what allows me to not get sucked up into the things of this world. My current schedule is intense. I'm always on the go. And without the reality of your relationship with God, your life will crush you, and all of a sudden you'll be burnt out. Burnout is illegal for a Christian! I believe we can raise up a generation of Christians who burn up for Jesus because we're so on fire with His love and truth. I believe we can raise up a generation of Christians who don't compromise. I believe we can raise up a generation of Christians who go about doing good, just as Jesus went about doing good . . . and He healed them all!

. . . how God anointed Jesus of Nazareth with the Holy Spirit and with power, who went about doing good and healing all who were oppressed by the devil, for God was with Him.

—ACTS 10:38

I believe we can raise up the reality of who God created us to be so that we would not be a people who are sucked up into the world. We don't have to see another minister fall. Jesus is beautiful, and we are created in His image. If we see who we were created to be, we will live in a place of relationship, a place of intimacy, an awesome place where we become like Him because we see Him as He is.

> Beloved, now we are children of God, and it has not appeared as yet what we will be. We know that when He appears, we will be like Him, because we will see Him just as He is.
>
> —1 John 3:2, nasb

The simplicity of the gospel is the truth of God getting in our hearts so that when Satan whispers lies in our ears, he is exposed, and we are fortified by the truth. When the truth gets in us, his lies have no access to our soul.

> For the weapons of our warfare are not carnal but mighty in God for pulling down strongholds, casting down arguments and every high thing that exalts itself against the knowledge of God, bringing every thought into captivity to the obedience of Christ.
>
> —2 Corinthians 10:4–5

> The lamp of the body is the eye. If therefore your eye is good, your whole body will be full of light.
>
> —Matthew 6:22

It's all about relationship, intimacy, and the stronghold of the Lord taking dominion over our minds. When Jesus sets up camp in our hearts, it's as if we have a "No Vacancy" sign on our foreheads, because truth has possessed us. Once He has possessed us, no one can dilute the gospel or take Him out of us. The Bible says that the same Holy Spirit who dwelled in Jesus dwells in us.

> But if the Spirit of Him who raised Jesus from the dead dwells in you, He who raised Christ from the dead will also give life to your mortal bodies through His Spirit who dwells in you.
>
> —ROMANS 8:11

Every believer has the same Holy Spirit; it's just a matter of whether we are willing to submit to His Spirit in us. Are you willing to lay down everything so that you can have intimacy and a relationship with the King? Mighty men and women of God can't afford to have anything compete with their intimacy with the Lord.

> No soldier in active service entangles himself in the affairs of everyday life, so that he may please the one who enlisted him as a soldier.
>
> —2 TIMOTHY 2:4, NASB

Nothing should come between us and our Father. Our lives are the outward display of our relationships with God. Grace is the divine inspiration of God upon our hearts, with the outward reflection of God upon our lives. Some people say that people should be able to see God's reflection in us. But the Bible doesn't say to arise and reflect—it says to arise and shine! It's a shine coming from the inside, not from the outside. When our eye is singular and our lamp is burning, it's not from the outside—it's Christ in us, shining through us.

Many in the body of Christ have not understood their transition from sinner to saint when they became born again. Some pastors even teach that you're always going to struggle with sins, and that you're always going to miss it. However, that's not the truth. The last thing I want to do is miss it. When I sin, I quickly repent and get straight with God. But I'm not thinking that I'm always going to miss it—because if I do that, then I already have a failure mentality. I'm almost certain to fail again and again if that's what I believe will happen. But I choose to believe what God's Word says instead.

Jesus overcame the power of sin for us on the cross. I'm dead to sin and alive to Christ and righteousness. My life isn't geared by my performance; my life is geared by His performance. I am in love with God, and everywhere I go that love is apparent. I'm not boasting in anything—I am secure in God's ability to keep me. I am consumed with God's ability to keep me more than I am consumed with the fear of Satan's ability to deceive me. My *doing* for Him is a by-product of my *being* with Him. People used to say to me, "Oh, I see. You must be brand-new because you're on fire!" Do you know that way of thinking is a demonic strategy? It doesn't matter if you have been a Christian for three days or thirty years—you should be on fire! Jesus hasn't changed. He is still the same, and we should be too.

Jesus Christ is the same yesterday and today and forever.

—HEBREWS 13:8, NASB

After a year of being a Christian, I was in a hospital praying for someone, and I watched that person get up off of his deathbed. The head nurse was there, and she came to me and said, "Oh, how long have you been a Christian?"

I began to tell her my testimony.

She said, "You need to slow down, son. This is a marathon not a sprint." That sounds great, but it's not in the Bible. As Christians our lives are neither a marathon nor a sprint. Our lives are a race. We're in a race! I get that we want people to run well and finish well, but it is the grace and mercy of God that enables us to run hard and finish well. It's my love relationship and intimacy with God. So instead of pointing out someone else's run, walk out the reality of your own relationship with God. What is your relationship with Jesus like? If you are too busy for a relationship with Jesus, then you are in trouble. The Christian life isn't about your super amazing giftedness. Gifts are given; fruit is grown. The gifts and calling of God are without repentance.

> For the gifts and the calling of God are irrevocable.
>
> —Romans 11:29

It's about relationship with Jesus. Some people can walk in great and powerful giftings, but behind closed doors they're different people. There has to be something different about us that is way above doing miracles. See, if I can teach you about who you are in Christ, the fruit of your life will be produced. Sonship is the priority, and the miraculous is a by-product of sonship—not the focal point. There is a difference between saying you know God and knowing for certain that God knows you. If miracles are your target, then you might end up walking in the gifts, but you won't see the need to repent to walk in them—and that's dangerous. In the Book of Matthew, Jesus said, "Not everyone who says to Me, 'Lord, Lord,' shall enter the kingdom of heaven." Not all that glitters is gold. In that day many will point to their gifts as proof of relationship, but He will say, "Depart from Me. I never knew you."

> Not everyone who says to Me, "Lord, Lord," shall enter the kingdom of heaven, but he who does the will of My Father in heaven. Many will say to Me in that day, "Lord, Lord, have we not prophesied in Your name, cast out demons in Your name, and done many wonders in Your name?" And then I will declare to them, "I never knew you; depart from Me, you who practice lawlessness!"
>
> —MATTHEW 7:21-23

If you gain who you are through your gifts, you will miss Him completely. What a shame it would be to gain your identity through the miracles you perform for God instead of knowing that you're one with God. You have to actually have and maintain your own relationship with God, or else you will become lopsided, pursuing the gifts at the expense of your character and your relationship with Jesus. The next thing you know, you're caught up in the praise of man instead of giving glory to God, and you're performing more miracles to try to validate your guilty conscience. You'll believe the lie that God is OK with the sin in your life because He is still performing miracles through you. Satan is not afraid of the gifts you carry or the signs and wonders you perform–he is afraid you'll discover who you are in Christ and become one with Him in a bona fide relationship.

I remember a time God told me, "Todd, you can have as much of Me as you want."

I said, "Lord, I want all of You! God, I want to know You. Father, I just need to know You. Father, I am asking You to show me who You are so I can see who I was created to be, because You created me in Your image."

Some people say, "God, I want less of me and more of You." They base this statement on what John the Baptist said in John 3:30: "He must increase, but I must decrease." But Christians take this verse out of context when they apply it to themselves. See, John the Baptist said that because he was exiting an Old Testament reality and entering a New Testament reality. He was really saying that he and the Law must decrease and that Jesus, righteousness, and truth must increase. He was getting out of the way so that the new covenant would come. When Christians take that verse out of context and apply it to themselves, they're mistaken. God doesn't want you to decrease; He wants you to completely surrender. God doesn't want you gone; He wants all of you completely covered by all of Him. If He wanted you gone, He would just kill you.

Now, he *does* want our carnal thinking to be completely gone. He wants us to have our minds renewed, and He wants us to set our minds on things above, to think the way He thinks. A full surrender of your whole life is what He wants. He wants all of you, not less of you! He wants all of you so that He can take up full occupancy of all you are and you can fully represent Him on the earth. It's an increase of Him all across the board. Once you belong to Jesus, you're a new creation. The old you is completely dead, not just on the decrease. The new you is alive to God—and that should never be on the decrease. It's God's pleasure to give you more of Himself. It's His pleasure to give you the kingdom.

> Do not fear, little flock, for it is your Father's good pleasure to give you the kingdom.
>
> —LUKE 12:32

You know, the first whole year of my first home Bible study, I didn't have anything else to talk about except for Ephesians chapter 1. People would come to my house and ask what we were going to talk about that time, and I would say, "You know what I have found, guys? God wants to give to us the spirit of wisdom, revelation, and knowledge of Him."

> . . . that the God of our Lord Jesus Christ, the Father of glory, may give to you a spirit of wisdom and of revelation in the knowledge of Him.
>
> —EPHESIANS 1:17, NASB

"Yeah, but we talked about that last time," they would say. I cycled through people after people after people, who would come and then stop coming. See, when I read Ephesians 1, it never gets old. The Word of God never gets old. Please don't ever think you already know it. We are all growing. None of us have arrived, but we are all growing in the reality of conforming to His image. We have to believe there is an open heaven wherever we go, and the only thing that can stop it is between our ears. Our mindsets have got to get in line with the truth in His Word. Our minds need to be set on God's interests, not man's interests.

Let's take a look at a passage of Scripture. Jesus was talking to Peter and His disciples about who the people were saying He was. Then He asked the disciples who *they* said He was.

> Simon Peter answered and said, "You are the Christ, the Son of the living God."
>
> Jesus answered and said to him, "Blessed are you, Simon Bar-Jonah, for flesh and blood has not revealed this to you, but My Father who is in heaven. And I also say to you that you are Peter, and on this rock I will build My church, and the gates of Hades shall not prevail against it. And I will give you the keys of the kingdom of heaven, and whatever you bind on earth will be bound in heaven, and whatever you loose on earth will be loosed in heaven."
>
> Then He commanded His disciples that they should tell no one that He was Jesus the Christ.
>
> From that time Jesus began to show to His disciples that He must go to Jerusalem, and suffer many things from the elders and chief priests and scribes, and be killed, and be raised the third day.
>
> Then Peter took Him aside and began to rebuke Him, saying, "Far be it from You, Lord; this shall not happen to You!"

But He turned and said to Peter, "Get behind Me, Satan! You are an offense to Me, for you are not mindful of the things of God, but the things of men."

Then Jesus said to His disciples, "If anyone desires to come after Me, let him deny himself, and take up his cross, and follow Me. For whoever desires to save his life will lose it, but whoever loses his life for My sake will find it."

—MATTHEW 16:16–25

When Jesus told Peter that it was the Father who had revealed who He was to Peter, He was essentially saying, "Simon, you didn't come up with that on your own—only God could've told you that." Jesus went on to explain that the church would be built on this same divine revelation: that He is the Christ, the Son of the living God, which can only be revealed by the Father. The gates of hell are resisted by that essential revelation. Then Jesus went on to tell them the plan for salvation—that He, the Christ, would be put to death and raised up on the third day. Upon hearing that news, Peter, being concerned with the interests of man, rather than the interests of God, rebuked the Lord for saying that. But Peter was wrong because his mind was set on the things of men, which is carnal thinking. The carnal mind is at war with God and always tries to shut down the gospel. But we have the mind of Christ.

. . . because the mind set on the flesh is hostile toward God; for it does not subject itself to the law of God, for it is not even able to do so.

—ROMANS 8:7, NASB

For "who has known the mind of the LORD that he may instruct Him?" But we have the mind of Christ.

—1 CORINTHIANS 2:16

If you have Jesus, then you have everything according to life and godliness, so release what's in you!

Grace and peace be multiplied to you in the knowledge of God and of Jesus our Lord; seeing that His divine power has granted to us everything pertaining to life and godliness, through the true knowledge of Him who called us by His own glory and excellence.

—2 PETER 1:2–3, NASB

We are either for Jesus, or we are against Him.
We either gather, or we scatter.

He who is not with Me is against Me; and he who does not gather with Me scatters.

—MATTHEW 12:30, NASB

I remember Dan telling me about an atheist who had a dream. In the dream he saw a huge field, and in the field there was a long fence that went right across the middle. On one side of the fence stood Jesus and all these people. On the other side was the devil and all these other people. The man could tell that the devil was attractive to people. See, in movies and books he is always displayed with a pitchfork, pointy ears, and a cape—but that is not how he looks. Satan comes across as attractive because he is a seducer. But in the dream this man could tell that he was darkness. The man knew he wasn't going to make a decision for Jesus or darkness, so he climbed up onto the fence. Suddenly all the people with Jesus disappeared, all the people with the devil disappeared, and he was sitting there all by himself. Everyone was gone. Then the devil came back and said, "There you are! I was looking for you!"

The man said, "Hey, I didn't choose Him, but I certainly didn't choose you!"

The devil said, "Sure you did! The fence belongs to me." As soon as that man woke up, he gave his life to Jesus.

You know, Jesus said, "I wish that you were either hot or cold." Jesus said it would be better to be hot or cold than lukewarm, because if you're lukewarm, He will spit you out of His mouth.

> So then, because you are lukewarm, and neither cold nor hot, I will vomit you out of My mouth.
>
> —Revelation 3:16

People don't want to read that. There are a lot of things in the Bible that people don't want to read because it convicts them, but conviction is what we need. Wherever the Holy Spirit convicts, grace comes in to enable us to stand up under what God's Word calls us to. You see, we tend to avoid conviction and only listen to the stuff that makes us feel good. The Holy Spirit is the Comforter. God knew that we were going to be very uncomfortable, so He gave us the Comforter.

And I will pray the Father, and he shall give you another Comforter, that he may abide with you for ever.

—John 14:16, kjv

You are required to depend upon the Holy Spirit to walk out your faith. Christianity cannot be lived out except by relationship with the Holy Spirit. Without Him it's just a book. The world thinks it's just a book anyway. Some say it is full of contradictions, but the truth is, when you read it in the Holy Spirit, there's not one contradiction. It meshes together like an amazing puzzle.

I sought the Lord about that passage of Scripture where He talked about hot or cold. I said, "But, Lord, at least the people who are warm know You and go to church."

He said, "No, Todd. You were ice cold, and I switched you to hot, and all you do is burn. But people who are warm damage the world around them. That's why it's so dangerous."

Being lukewarm damages the world. Being lukewarm is having a form of godliness but denying the power thereof.

> . . . having a form of godliness but denying its power.
> And from such people turn away!
>
> —2 Timothy 3:5

Oftentimes people don't walk out what they quote in Scripture because they don't really believe it. The Holy Spirit wants to empower us. We say things such as, "I'm unworthy." Really? Listen very carefully: Satan is known for one thing that he repeatedly attacks Christians with, and that's the lie that you're not worth it, that you're worthless. Why? Because he is worthless. If I were to sell you a car and tell you I wanted $5,000 for the car, but you knew that it was only worth $500, would you give me $5,000? No way! If you were house shopping, and I showed you a house and told you I wanted $10,000,000, and you knew it was only worth $100,000, would you give me $10,000,000? No, you wouldn't! Well, if in the world the value of something is always determined by the price that's paid for it, and heaven went bankrupt to get you back, how dare you look in the mirror and say you're worthless!

Jesus said the two greatest commandments are to love the Lord God with all your heart, soul, mind, and strength, and to love your neighbors as yourself.

> "And you shall love the Lord your God with all your heart, with all your soul, with all your mind, and with all your strength." This is the first commandment. And the second, like it, is this: "You shall love your neighbor as yourself." There is no other commandment greater than these.
>
> —Mark 12:30–31

When I love God with everything that I am, I can look in the mirror and love myself. And if I can't love myself, then I can't love you. It would be false love, fake love. I could tell you that I love you, but I would have secrets and wouldn't be able to have true fellowship with you. The Bible says to walk in the light as He is in the light; then we can have fellowship with one another.

> But if we walk in the light as He is in the light, we have fellowship with one another, and the blood of Jesus Christ His Son cleanses us from all sin.
>
> −1 John 1:7

So, if I am clean and clear before God in my heart and my soul and my mind, then I am in fellowship with Him, and I can have fellowship with you. However, if I am living in lies, then I am living in darkness and won't be able to view myself correctly. Then shame, fear, and condemnation come in and become my identity so that I hide behind a mask around others. If I am hiding stuff, I can't allow anyone to get too close to me, which means the only relationships I can have are surface relationships and fake connections, but nothing real or deep or genuine. We can't afford to have surface relationships with people. We need to walk in the light as He is in the light, in unity with Him and one another.

I don't see a cost to living out the gospel. You know what the price is? Jesus paid it. All God is asking you to do is to give up something you were never created to be in the first place. He didn't create you for you; He created you for Him.

See, we love ourselves in the wrong way. When God created me, He created me to become a vessel of His love. When I see who I really am, I become a vessel of His love. God is love!

He who does not love does not know God, for God is love.

—1 John 4:8

And Jesus was the visible image of the invisible God.

He is the image of the invisible God, the firstborn over all creation.

—Colossians 1:15

He was the express image of the Father.

And He is the radiance of His glory and the exact representation of His nature, and upholds all things by the word of His power. When He had made purification of sins, He sat down at the right hand of the Majesty on high.

—Hebrews 1:3, NASB

He is the way, the truth, and the life, and no one comes to the Father except by Him.

Jesus said to him, "I am the way, and the truth, and the life; no one comes to the Father but through Me."

—John 14:6, NASB

I'm so glad He didn't say, "No one comes to heaven except by Me." Heaven needs to be our destination but not our mission. Heaven is the destination of our lives here; it's a place where we get to go be with Jesus for all eternity. But in this present life our mission statement isn't just to get to heaven but for heaven to get into us, by agency of the Holy Spirit, so that we can do the works Jesus called us to. Our mission is 1 John 3:8–to destroy the works of the devil as Jesus did.

> He who sins is of the devil, for the devil has sinned from the beginning. For this purpose the Son of God was manifested, that He might destroy the works of the devil.
>
> —1 JOHN 3:8

We don't want to bypass an encounter with the Father here on earth. If we don't realize when we get born again that God is our Father, we'll be headed to heaven, but we'll live like hell with a mindset of an orphan until we get there. We will barely make it in by the skin of our teeth–and we don't have skin on our teeth. That's a great loss! It's not about just barely making it into heaven; it's about being confident and having confidence now to approach the throne of grace in time of need. Eternal life starts now, here on earth, because knowing the Father is eternal life.

> Let us therefore come boldly to the throne of grace, that we may obtain mercy and find grace to help in time of need.
>
> —HEBREWS 4:16

> This is eternal life, that they may know You, the only true God, and Jesus Christ whom You have sent.
>
> —JOHN 17:3, NASB

Let me ask you something: When is the last time you didn't need Jesus? We have to be heavenly minded so that we are earthly incredible.

Your life can become a walking, talking powerhouse of the gospel so that the powerless will come to know Jesus because of you. That's kingdom living! Over the course of the following three chapters, I want to encourage your faith by sharing a few testimonies with you. These are just a few amazing stories out of thousands I have personally experienced in my daily walk with Christ. To Jesus be all the glory!

Chapter 11

The Story of Tanner

One day I went to Atlanta to speak at Bethel Atlanta Church. I arrived a couple nights early and met up with some friends there to go out to eat. We shared the gospel with some waiters and waitresses there, and then we went back to the hotel. The next day, I went to work out, talked to more people, and more people received healing in their bodies and got saved at the gym. My assistant at that time was a guy named William. Later that afternoon William and I went back to the hotel to shower and get ready to go out again. As we were walking down the hallway of the hotel, I saw a woman getting ice from the ice machine. I stopped to ask her if she knew how much Jesus loved her. She said she did and thanked me. Right then I received a word of knowledge.

I said, "Do you or someone you know have a torn rotator cuff?"

She replied, "It's my boyfriend."

"Oh wow. OK. Can we call him?"

"Oh, he's here. He's in our room."

"May I go pray for him?"

"I don't think so," she said. "He doesn't want anything to do with God."

"That's OK. I'd still like to pray for his shoulder."

"Well, I can try to get him to come out here if he's willing, but I'm warning you, he probably won't come out here."

"Yeah, that's OK. Do you have an aunt that has a mental disorder? Like she's bipolar?"

"Oh my gosh! Yes, I have an aunt that has a severe bipolar disorder!"

"If we pray right now, God will touch her right now!" I said.

"OK!"

We began to pray, and she was overwhelmed with the specifics of the word of knowledge I was getting. After we prayed, I told her how much Jesus loves her.

She was excited and said, "Let me go talk to my boyfriend and see if I can get him to come out here!"

Sure enough her boyfriend got out of bed and came down the hall to talk to me. He was a big guy. He didn't look happy at all to have been woken up to come talk about God with some man he didn't know.

"Hey, man, how are you doing?" I said.

"What's all this about?"

"Well, I heard in my heart that someone really close to your girlfriend has a torn rotator cuff, and I guess that's you."

"Yeah. OK. So what?" He was tired and grumpy.

"May I pray for you?"

"I don't care."

I put my hand on his left shoulder and began to pray. Then afterwards I asked him to check his shoulder.

He lifted up his arm and said, "Oh my God! What is going on right now?" He started freaking out because his shoulder was healed, and he didn't understand how that could be possible.

I said, "Jesus just healed your shoulder!"

"This is not possible!"

"No, it is possible!"

Right then I received another word of knowledge. "You had a grandmother you really cared about when you were little. She loved the Lord, and yet she still got ill and died, even though she prayed desperately to God to live. When she died, you were very angry with God. You knew how much your grandmother loved God, and you decided that if God wouldn't answer your grandmother's prayers, then He wasn't real. You've been mad at Him ever since. But you know He's real, and you know He just healed your shoulder. What do you think your grandmother would be saying right now? She is with Jesus in heaven. What do you think she would say to you right now? She would tell you to run to the Lord! Are you ready to give your life back to Jesus?"

He was overcome with emotion, "Yeah, I am."

We prayed right then, and he gave his life to Jesus.

I was still planning to leave the hotel, but they weren't ready to say goodbye to me yet, so they got in the elevator with me to go downstairs. Now, I knew that the girlfriend was a Christian and had compromised her faith to live with this guy. However, since her boyfriend had just received Jesus, I wanted to encourage them to live holy from here on out. So I decided to share my testimony about Jackie and me, and how God had convicted us about living together unmarried and brought us into the purity of covenant.

"That's an amazing story, man!" he said.

"No, it's not just a story. It's a testimony, which means God wants to do it again—and He wants to do it with you!"

I told them I loved them and gave them hugs, then left to go out. (A little later that year, they contacted our ministry to let us know they were getting married.)

William and I left the hotel and went to a Texas Roadhouse restaurant. Another friend named Robert met up with us to have dinner. We were talking, and William went ahead of us to go inside and get us a table. As Robert and I were walking in the restaurant, a waitress came out, plowed right into me, then ran past me. I said, "Hey! Can I talk to you for a minute?"

"What?" she screamed. She was crying and clearly having a really bad day.

"Can I give you a hug?"

"Why?"

"Because you really need one right now."

"OK," she said, and she gave me a little pat on the back.

"Are you OK?"

"No! I'm not OK! I'm having a horrible day!" She began to explain her shortcomings.

"You want to be a psychologist, don't you?"

"What? How did you know that?"

"You want to be a psychologist, and you want to go to college, but you don't have the money, and neither does your mom, but your mom wants you to be one too."

She began to scream and freak out. "You're crazy!" she exclaimed.

"Is it true?"

"Yes! How do you know that?"

I told her about Jesus. Her mom was a Christian too and had been praying for her.

She said, "I don't want to hear this right now."

"Wait! God is so interested in you that He knows exactly what career path you want to take, and He knows exactly what is stopping you from that. I think that's something worth considering."

"I don't believe you." She was angry.

"Here's what I'm going to do: I'm going to tell you exactly what just happened at our hotel just before we arrived here, and then I am going to have my friend William come out here and tell you word for word what I am about to say to you."

She said, "OK."

So I told her about the testimony in the hotel and then called for William to come out. I said, "Tell her what happened at the hotel."

He told her word for word what I had just said.

"Oh my gosh! This is not happening right now!" She broke down and started bawling.

"Honey," I said, "you've been running away from God. You used to go to church and sing in the choir, but it's been years, and your mom has been praying for you this entire time. Do you know what will open the door for you to go to college? You giving your life back to Jesus and letting Him open that door for you."

"I don't have anything else to give."

"Well, Jesus will take you!"

She cried, "OK!"

Then we prayed, and she got born again. Then she gave me her contact information so I could give it to the people at the church I was about to go speak at. We always try to get people plugged into a local church if there's an opportunity for that.

We went inside to eat, and our waiter came up to the table to get our drink order. His name was Tanner. I told him how much Jesus loves him.

He said, "Cool, bro. I'm glad you found your path."

I said, "Well, He's more than a path."

"Well, I'm not very religious, but I am spiritual."

"Jesus loves you so much, and I'm just glad I got to meet you today."

"Man, you're pretty cool."

I said, "Well, I just appreciate you because you're real open, and you're spiritual. You just need a real Spirit!"

He said, "Whoa, dude. OK." Then he took our drink order and walked away.

When Tanner returned to our table, I received another word of knowledge in my heart—he had broken his left wrist playing on monkey bars when he was little.

I said, "This may sound crazy, man, but did you break your left wrist playing on monkey bars when you were nine years old?"

"How did you know that, man?"

I began to talk to him about the Holy Spirit that I have inside of me.

"No way, dude! That's amazing! What else do you know about me, man?"

"Sit down, bro."

I began telling him my testimony and shared the gospel with him.

He listened, but they were busy, and he had to run to check on some other tables.

Later he returned and said, "Man, how did you know those things about me?"

"When you walked away, the Lord spoke to me and said that tonight was going to be your last night. Tanner, you don't have any time left, bro." I began to tear up. I was losing it. "You don't have any time left, Tanner. The Lord told me tonight is your last night."

He burst into tears. "I just left rehab early, and I was planning on going out to have my last hurrah tonight." He meant he was planning to party and purposely overdose on drugs.

"Oh my gosh, Tanner! This is the Lord! You know this is the Lord intervening on your behalf! Tanner, you need Jesus! Are you ready?"

He said yes and prayed with us, right there at the table, to surrender his life to Jesus.

Tanner said, "Man, I haven't cried like this in so long."

"You have a mom that has been praying for you."

"Yeah, I know she's been praying for me."

I said, "Listen, you need to call her."

Right then he received a text from his mom, asking what time she was supposed to pick him up. You see, his original plan was to tell her that he wasn't getting off work until late and then to go out and party with his friend instead. They were going to go shoot up heroin. But now he was saved, and he wasn't going to do that.

So Tanner called his mom, "Hey, Mom, I'm here with some new friends, and I just wanted to call to tell you I just got saved."

I could hear his mom screaming with joy in the background, and I asked if I could talk to her. He handed me the phone.

"How did you get to my son? How did you do this?"

"I need you to know that Tanner is legitimately born again right now. So many things have transpired right here at the table. But you're his mom, and I just want to say, 'Well done, Mom!' for praying and not giving up." I was crying—we all were crying. Then I said, "Will you do me a favor? I'm speaking at Bethel Church here in Atlanta tomorrow. Will you come and bring your son?"

She said, "I'm there!"

I said, "Tanner, will you come?"

"Of course I'll come!"

The next morning when I got to the church, it was packed with people. I saw Tanner there with a young lady and his mom. The young lady had been severely hurt in life and had gone through some really dark things. After worship was over, I got up to speak, and the Holy Spirit told me to take up an offering for Tanner's mom. So I shared Tanner's testimony with the church and told them I felt like we were supposed to take up an offering for Tanner's mom because of all the money she had paid for rehab programs for Tanner and all the credit card debt and financial strain she had been under. I looked over at Tanner's mom, and she had completely lost composure. She was crying and so overwhelmed that God would bless her like that. Suddenly people from all over the congregation began running up to the front to put money on the stage for Tanner's mom, hugging her and Tanner and rejoicing with her. She was given about seven thousand dollars from people in the church.

Then I turned to the young lady who came with Tanner, and I prayed for her. She got delivered and saved right then and gave her life to Jesus also.

Tanner said, "Wow, man! This is so cool! It feels like my birthday!"

I said, "It is, bro! Your first day as a born-again believer, living for Jesus!"

The entire church was rocked by the Lord's goodness and faithfulness that morning.

Chapter 12

The Story of Rocky

One day I traveled to Durban, South Africa, to meet the elders and pastor of a local church there. The plan was to do a meet and greet with the elders and then host a two-day training and outreach event for their church. During the meeting with the elders, I shared a testimony from a church service that had just taken place the night before. The testimony I shared was about a man at the meeting who was angry with God. I had a word of knowledge that the man blamed God for his wife's death, so I told the man that Jesus didn't take his wife. I began praying over him, and the Holy Spirit touched him. He fell into my chest weeping and surrendered his life to Jesus. As I was telling the elders this story, something remarkable happened. The Holy Spirit came in with fresh fire and began to overtake the meeting and touch the church leaders. Bodies were flipping and flying to the floor. I hadn't done anything but share a testimony. It was a sovereign move of the Holy Spirit on the elders. He was touching those leaders and preparing that church for His presence and outpouring in that region. They recognized this was the gospel with power.

After the meeting we all went down to the pier to do outreach ministry with the Durban locals. While we were walking along the pier, I saw a guy wearing glasses who stood out to me. I found out later his name was Rocky.

I said, "Hey, buddy, Jesus loves you!"

He pulled down his glasses and said, "Are you talking to me?"

"Yes, I am. I just want you to know Jesus loves you and He sees you!" I knew in my heart I needed to grab his hand. "May I have your hand?"

"Yeah!" He grabbed my hand in anger and tried to break it, but it didn't work.

I kept going. "You have a son that you don't have a relationship with, and God wants to restore that relationship! You also have three businesses. God is going to land on two of them, and those two are going to be the ones that you are to focus on." Then I gave him words of knowledge about his family. Rocky just sat there and gasped. Then he surrendered his life to Jesus.

After he was saved and at peace, he asked if I was OK, as he was concerned that he had broken my hand. He didn't break anything—the devil was broken off of his life that day. I put Rocky in connection with the elders so he could get plugged into the local church.

One year later I was at the airport in Johannesburg, South Africa, waiting to board a flight to Durban, where I was going to be ministering at that same church for the second time. Our flight was delayed, and we were told we would have to wait an extra forty-five minutes before takeoff. I noticed an Indian man in line, complaining out loud that he didn't understand why there was a delay and that he really needed to get home. I didn't say anything to him, as I was praying in the spirit under my breath. (Just a side note here: I pray in tongues every opportunity I get—not necessarily because anything needs urgent prayer, but simply because I want to stay in communion with God and build up my spirit man as much as possible. I encourage you to use your downtime to pray and get connected to the Lord whenever you're able.)

Finally it was time to board the aircraft. I had an aisle seat three rows back on the plane. After I sat down, the Indian man walked on board. Immediately the countenances of the people on the plane changed, and I realized he was someone really well-known to them. He was wearing a suit and tie and looked like a wealthy businessman. For the sake of his privacy I will refer to him as Eli from here on out. His seat was by mine, but he took one look at me, turned, and asked the flight attendant to be seated elsewhere. Fortunately the only other seat available was the aisle seat across from me, so he was still right beside me.

As we began to ascend, I told him, "Hey, I just want to tell you Jesus loves you."

He said, "Thank you."

Other people were trying to get his attention to talk to him, so I began to share the gospel with the flight attendants and pray for them. One lady, who already knew the Lord, was in need of healing, so I prayed for her and her right shoulder was healed. Then the Lord spoke to me and told me that the man across from me had a heart issue. Instinctively I knew it was his actual heart that wasn't functioning properly. So I asked him if he had any issues with his heart, but he denied there was any problem.

I said, "What do you do?"

"I'm a businessman. Many people know me because I'm in the newspaper a lot. Some people write bad things about me. What do you do?"

"I'm in business too!"

"What kind of business do you do?"

"Well, I'm about my Father's business."

"Who is your Father?"

I said, "I'm so glad you asked!" Then I began to share the gospel with him.

He said, "Well then, we don't believe the same way." He was Hindu.

"That's OK. It doesn't matter. I just wanted to share my life story with you."

Eli listened intently as I shared my testimony with him. He said he had never heard anything like it, but that my story seemed very significant.

I told him again how much Jesus loves him.

As the plane began to descend in Durban, he asked, "How did you know about my heart problem?"

"God is my Father, and He speaks to me."

"This is very interesting! Will you pray for my heart?"

"Yes!" I put my hand on his heart, and his chest became very hot.

"My chest feels very warm. I feel peace."

"Isn't that amazing? Jesus is that peace."

Then he told me that when we landed, his assistant would get my bags and that I would not have to carry them. That wasn't necessary, but I could tell that his having control was a big part of his role as a prominent businessman. Everyone around us was astounded that he was even talking to me with my dreadlocks. When we disembarked the plane, his assistant took my bag. Right then the Lord showed me that his assistant used to be a Christian but became a Hindu. He also showed me that he had dreamed of being a professional rugby player, but that dream crashed and burned when he tore his ACL on the field. He thought the Lord had done it to him on purpose to keep him from something he really wanted to do, and now he was an assistant.

I said, "Let me tell you this right now: you used to be a Christian, but you turned your back on God because you thought that He was the One who tore your ACL in your left knee on the rugby field."

He looked at me in shock.

Eli said, "Is this true?" His assistant confirmed that it was true, and his boss said, "Then let this man pray for you! His God will heal your knee!"

I prayed for the man and, sure enough, the Lord healed his knee. He began to cry, and as we went on our way to the baggage claim area, I told him he needed to give his life back to the Lord. He said he knew and he would.

The pastor from the church I was going to be speaking at met me at the baggage claim and recognized the man I was with from the newspapers. They talked for a moment, and Eli decided he would come to the service to hear me speak. When we got in the car, the pastor told me that the guy I met on the plane was well known for being a shady character, and if he were to get saved, it would be a total miracle!

That evening, when I went up front to speak, a girl came up to me on the stage and said, "You saved my father."

"What? How? What do you mean?"

"Do you remember the guy you met on the pier with the glasses?"

"Yeah!"

"That was my father." She began to cry. "That was my dad. I never had a dad until you met my dad. Then he became a dad to me."

Her mom came up to us, and I knew it was Rocky's wife before she even came up to us. I said, "You're Rocky's wife!"

"I am," she said. "May I tell you what happened to him?"

"Yes, of course!" I said.

At this point she already had a microphone and began to share the testimony with me and the entire congregation. Most of the church was already aware of the story.

"Well, first of all, I want you to know that Rocky passed away two weeks ago. He was out boogie boarding and had a heart attack. That day you met him on the pier last year was going to be his last day. He had just left a suicide note at our house and had planned to go throw himself off the pier into the shallow end and kill himself. In the suicide note he explained that the businesses were failing, he had no relationship with his son, and that he was not a good father. Then he said goodbye and signed off. However, later that day, he came stumbling into the house with sand all in his hair and told us he had met a man with dreadlocks on the pier. He said that right before he was going to jump, he saw you and prayed, 'God, if You're real, have that man tell me that You love me and that You see me.' Right after he prayed, you walked up and said those exact words to him."

She went on to explain that over the course of that year, he became best friends with his son and raised up kingdom business leaders all over Durban. Both of his businesses are still thriving and have provided their family money to live on for the rest of their lives.

Eli, the businessman I met on the plane, was there. He was listening intently to the testimony about Rocky. After the meeting he texted the guy I was staying with and asked if I would be willing to meet with his son. He said his son had schizophrenia, and he wanted me to pray for him. I agreed to meet with them, so we planned to meet at a restaurant later.

I arrived at the restaurant early, and they were running late, so I began to pray for the waitstaff. When Eli came in, he motioned me over to a table. He let me know that his son would be another thirty minutes, but he wanted us to go ahead and talk. So we began talking and getting to know each other better. All of a sudden he said we had to get up and move. I asked why, and he said it was because the reporter who talked bad about him in the newspapers was right there by us, only one chair away, and was listening to our conversation.

I said, "No way, really?"

"Yeah, we have to move."

"Well, that is not a coincidence." So I got up and went over to the guy to speak with him. I said, "Hey there. You're a reporter, right?"

"Yeah." He was caught.

"Man, is it true that you have a herniated disc and sciatic nerve damage down your left leg right now?"

"Uh, yeah!

"Are you a Christian?"

"Yeah."

"Can I pray for you?"

He agreed, we prayed, and he was instantly healed. Then I said, "Isn't it amazing how much God loves you? And you see that man over there? He's a good man; he just doesn't know it yet. He needs Jesus."

"He *does* need Jesus."

"Why don't you *give* him Jesus then?"

"I get it." And he got up and left.

Finally Eli's son arrived at the restaurant. As we were sitting down together and talking, the son started hearing voices. Eli said, "I really need help with my son. Will you please pray for him?"

"I will not pray for your son unless I can share the gospel with him."

"OK. Go ahead."

I shared the gospel and my testimony of how God delivered me of mental turmoil. I told him, "My Jesus will fix you."

The son said, "I want your Jesus."

We prayed, and the son was born again right in front of his father. The demonic oppression he was under lifted, the voices stopped, and the son was completely set free from schizophrenia.

His dad looked at him in the eyes and could tell he was well. He was deeply moved. Then he dropped his head and said, "I have been trying to find peace, and I used to have peace a long time ago, but I have no peace anymore."

"Jesus will give you peace, but you have to surrender your life!"

"What does that even look like?"

"It looks like putting your faith in Jesus alone and turning your back on every Hindu god you've ever known. Pledge your allegiance to Jesus the King!"

"I will do it to have peace."

"You'll do it to have eternity. This is eternal life."

Then Eli gave his life to Jesus. He was so overwhelmed with joy that he began calling people from his office to come meet us to get prayer. Many people came and were touched by Jesus that day.

Later he wanted me to come to another meeting, this time at his house, to talk to his wife and family. He had me picked up in a Rolls-Royce they called "The Ghost." As soon as I found out the nickname for the car, I thought, "Yes! The *Holy* Ghost!" I shared my heart with the driver on the way to the house, and he got saved. When we arrived at the house, Eli's wife greeted me and told me her mom was in the hospital with a lung condition. I told her we could call and pray for the woman on the phone. All the pain and shortness of breath subsided, and she was healed also. Then we sat down, and I could tell that Eli was at odds with his wife because he had left the house a Hindu and returned home a Christian. He got up and left the room.

His wife looked at me and said, "Listen. My children can worship a cow, a horse, a tree, or a cricket. I'm not going to tell them that they have to worship your Jesus."

I began to share my testimony with her, as she had not heard it before.

"My husband is claiming that he has changed, but it would take a lot of work to change that man."

I thought to myself, "There's change necessary in front of me."

She began to tell me that something horrible happened to her when she was a little girl, so she struggled with getting past fear. I explained to her that there is no fear in love and love is in Jesus!

I said, "I want you to pray with me and accept the Lord because Jesus will take this fear away from you!" She decided to surrender to Jesus, and she was radically born again right then.

I returned home from South Africa, completely astounded at what the Lord had done in such a small period of time. Jesus is amazing! He will accomplish great things through you when you give Him everything.

Take it from Rocky: life is short—leave a legacy!

Chapter 13

The Story of Jesse

In 2013 I traveled to Tulsa, Oklahoma, to speak at a men's conference, A Call to Arms, at Rhema Bible Church. I had a little downtime before the conference, so I decided to go to the guitar store to take a look around. I didn't really need anything, but I thought I would just grab a guitar and see if I could play with whoever was there practicing. When I got there, I went to the acoustic room to play, but there was no one in there. When I came back out, I saw a tall, thin guy with long hair, playing in the electric guitar section. He had headphones on, and most of the sound was coming through those instead of the amplifier. Still, from what little I was able to hear, I could tell he was an extremely talented electric guitar player.

I went up to him and said, "Hey, bro, how are you?"

He said, "What's up, man?"

"You're really good! Do you play in a band?"

"Nah, I just play for fun." Then he put his headphones back on and started playing again.

I tapped him on the shoulder and said "Hey, can I show you a friend of mine that plays music?"

"Yeah, if you want to."

I pulled out my phone and showed him some Christian rock bands that I knew of.

He said, "I'm no Christian, bro."

"That's OK. Do you mind listening to this for a minute? Because I think you'll like it."

He listened for a minute and said, "Yeah, they're really good. I'm not that good."

"Yes, you are! You're that good." I began to encourage him. I found out his name was Jesse, and I asked him if I could share my story with him and where I came from.

"Sure."

So I shared my testimony of how I came out of a life of drug addiction and all kinds of junk. When I got to the end, he just said, "That's pretty cool, man. That's pretty cool."

"Thanks, bro."

Then he said, "You seem like a pretty cool guy. Do you want to talk?"

I said, "Yes, of course, I'd love to talk."

"What are you doing here in Tulsa?"

"I'm actually here to speak at a men's conference about Jesus."

"Oh, cool deal. Is that what you do?"

"Yes, but I also speak to people everywhere I go, and you're one of those people today."

He said, "Cool, man. Come with me."

Then he went over to the keyboard and started playing the piano. He was really good at that too–basically this guy could play any instrument. He had a gift.

"Man, you're like amazing! You have such a gift!"

Then, out of the blue, he said, "You know, my dad shot himself in the head a couple years ago. I found him. But it's OK. I'm good."

"What did you just say?"

"Yeah, I found my dad. He committed suicide. He was on drugs too. But that's OK."

I said, "Oh bro, I'm so sorry!"

"That's OK. I play music now, man! I'm all good."

Essentially what he was saying was that music was his escape.

Right then the Holy Spirit gave me a word of knowledge. "Bro, your back is messed up."

"Yeah. Wait, how do you know that?"

"God told me."

"How did God tell you?"

"Just let me pray for your back." Then I prayed for God to heal his back.

"What the **** is that, bro? What is happening right now? Oh my gosh!"

"Check your back, bro."

"Oh my gosh!" He started to freak out because his back pain was gone.

I said, "What do you think of that, man?"

"That's amazing! Bro, I wish my girlfriend was here. She's religious like you. And she's really hurting . . . "

"She's got migraine headaches," I interrupted.

"How did you know that? Dude, this is so crazy!"

"Where is she?"

"She's next door at the store. She's with my ten-month-old little girl, and my mom is with her."

"Oh wow! Can we go over there and pray for her?"

He called his girlfriend on the phone and told her he had met some "religious guy" who knew about her migraine headaches and wanted to come pray for her. Then they hung up, and he said, "Yeah, let's go!"

Then we walked over to the store. His mom and girlfriend were waiting at the front of the store. The girlfriend gave me a weird look, then walked back to the women's section. Jesse went to talk to her. Then it was just me, his mom, and Jesse's little girl, who was sitting in the cart. I began to talk with Jesse's mom. She was astonished that he had opened up to me about his father and said that he never shares that with anyone. His dad had shot himself in the head with a double-barrel shotgun, and Jesse had found him afterwards.

She went on to tell me that she was a Christian and was surprised Jesse had allowed me to pray for him and talk to him about God. I told her God wanted to heal her back too. She said that would be great. Then she told me that Jesse was really hurting inside and not doing OK. He had been struggling with depression and suicidal thoughts. She also shared that he had gotten into some trouble, and they had to bail him out of jail.

I said, "May I pray for your back really quick? Then I'm going to go spend some time with Jesse and his girlfriend."

She said, "Sure! That would be wonderful!"

I prayed for her back, and she was healed. Then I walked to the back of the store, where Jesse and his girlfriend were standing at the checkout counter. I asked his girlfriend, "Would you do me a favor?"

"What?"

"Will you let me buy you clothes today? Just whatever you guys want to get, I'll get it."

"Why would you do that?" She looked at me like I was a lunatic.

Jesse said, "Bro, you don't have to do that."

"I want to! Will you let me? See most people, when they think of God, they think He's a thief because there's been money scandals in the church and all these different things. The truth is God loved us so much that He gave His Son, Jesus, for us. If I talk to you about God but fail to be generous and bless you, then how can I even say I know God?"

Jesse said, "Dude, you are something else! You're not buying me anything, but you can get my baby girl something if you want."

So I went to talk to the grandma, who originally planned to buy them some things that day. I told her what I wanted to do for them. We began to pick out some new clothes.

Jesse went outside to smoke a cigarette. He couldn't handle all that was happening. He and his girlfriend began to be afraid that there must be strings attached to my generosity.

No one does something for nothing—except the Lord. And the Lord lives in me. God didn't want to take anything from us; He did everything for us—no strings attached.

Grandma was thrilled! She told me Jesse needed clothes too and that she was going to buy him a few things, but she was limited financially.

I said, "I'll take care of it. Let's go on a shopping spree!"

She was beaming with excitement and exclaimed, "This is a miracle!"

We filled the cart up with a huge pile of new clothes for Jesse, his girlfriend, and their daughter. It was so fun! Once we gathered everything they needed, we went to the checkout counter. Our cashier happened to be trapped in the wrong lifestyle, and he was blown away that I was buying all these items for this young family. While we were talking, Jesse came back in and began to explain the whole story to our cashier.

He said, "Dude, let me tell you something, man. I don't even know this guy! He prayed for me, and my back got healed over there. Then he prayed for my girl's headaches, and I didn't tell him about any of those things! He just knows all this stuff! He's a Christian, and on top of all of that, he wants to buy all of these clothes for my family!"

I told him the Lord had told me to bless them. The cashier was stunned and asked where I was from. After I told him, he said, "Well, we don't have Christians like that around here!" (Wouldn't it be great if the whole body of Christ got a face-lift of love and generosity? What would it look like if the church developed a reputation for extravagant giving?)

I knew that this guy had a distorted self-image, so I told him, "Jesus loves you! I don't know if you know that for sure, but I'm here to tell you He does!"

The cashier started crying and was so overwhelmed that another employee had to take over the cash register. He couldn't even continue the conversation because God hit him so hard through generosity and love when he saw real love for people in action, with no strings attached.

When we were finished at the checkout counter, Jesse thanked me for everything and let me know he had to go back to the guitar store. He was still emotional and didn't know how to handle all that was happening.

His girlfriend said, "I still don't understand why you did all of this."

"Because God loves you guys."

She said a quick, "Yep," and went back to the guitar store with Jesse.

I asked the grandma what was going on with Jesse's girlfriend. She explained that she was just rattled because of her previous experience with religion, and she just couldn't believe I would do something like that for nothing in return. The grandma also said that Jesse had been coming to the guitar shop regularly for a couple months, ever since they had to sell his guitar and all of his equipment to bail him out of jail. They had to drive an hour to the shop just so he could play and have some relief. She said the guitar store was the only place he could find peace. Right then I said, "I'm going to buy him a guitar!"

"No, you're not. You can't," she said.

"Yes, I am. I can! I'm already going! What kind of guitar did he have?"

"I have no idea, but his girlfriend does."

When I walked in the guitar shop, his girlfriend saw me and let out a nettled, "What?"

"You think that there are strings attached here."

"Well, there has to be something."

"There's nothing. What kind of guitar did Jesse have? Was it something like this?" I pointed to one of many guitars on the wall.

"That's not the kind that he had, but that is the kind that he wants."

"So you're telling me that out of forty guitars on the wall, the one I just pointed to is the one that Jesse wants?"

"Yeah."

"I'm buying it for him."

"No, you're not." She walked away from me.

Meanwhile Jesse was across the shop playing the drums. I walked over to him and he took off his headphones,

"What, man? What do you want?" He was totally freaking out.

You see, everything important to him had been stolen. His father had committed suicide, and Jesse had been the one to find him dead. Music had been the only way for Jesse to escape the intense pain from that traumatic event, and then he lost that too. He was afraid to hope for anything else.

"Bro, I need you to come with me right now."

"What do you want, man?"

"I heard that you went to jail and had to pawn your guitar to post bail."

"How do you know all of this stuff?"

"Your mom told me that part."

"Oh my gosh, dude. Why did she tell you that?"

"Jesse, remember when I told you my story, of how I had been in prison? I pawned everything, bro. I ripped off everybody my whole life, and man, I just needed a break. And you know what I heard in my heart?" I took the guitar off the shelf and handed it to him.

"Dude! This is my favorite ******* guitar! You don't understand, bro. This is like my dream guitar! This is the best guitar ever! I won't even play it because it's my dream guitar!"

"Well, I'm buying it for you!"

"Shut up, man!" He handed it back to me.

"Bro! I'm being serious. The Lord spoke to me to buy you this guitar."

"Why are you saying this, man?"

"Because the Lord loves you, Jesse. He just wants to bless you so you know He loves you."

Jesse looked at me, "No one does this stuff, man! Nobody does this!"

"God does. He did it for us with His Son. Look, man, I understand you don't understand the whole Jesus thing. Maybe you're not ready for all of that, but I want to sow some seeds into your life. This guitar is going to be a seed. And I know you're going to play this like a champion!"

"Man, don't mess with me! Don't play with me right now."

"I'm not playing. I'm getting you this guitar! And we're going to walk out of this store, and it's going to be yours!"

"For real?"

"For real!"

We walked over to the counter, and the manager said, "It's Jesse, right?"

"Yeah, man, but I'm not going to be coming here anymore, man. Guess what?" He then shared the whole testimony of everything that had just happened.

The manager said, "I'm a Christian, bro, but I've never seen anything like this in my life. Are you serious?"

I said, "Yes!"

The manager started crying. Jesse was crying. I was crying. Then I told him we also needed a case for the guitar. We went over and picked out a case for the guitar. The guy still couldn't believe I was doing this for a young man I had just met, so he asked me, "What's your name?"

"My name doesn't matter. What matters is that Jesus is generous and He is not a thief. He's amazing! And God so loved the world that He gave us his only Son!"

> For God so loved the world that He gave His only begotten Son, that whoever believes in Him should not perish but have everlasting life.
>
> –John 3:16

He gave me a big hug.

I told Jesse I was sorry his dad did what he had done, but that he didn't have to end up like his dad.

"Oh! I'm not going down that road," Jesse said.

"There is only one road you need–it's Jesus. And when you're by yourself, just pray, 'God, I didn't know that You were real, but now I know You're real because I saw You in a man today, and I want You to be in my life.'"

"I got you, bro." And he gave me big hug.

We walked out of the store with Jesse's new guitar. His mom saw us and fell apart. Her voice quivered, "You really got him the guitar!"

Jesse's girlfriend was in the car. She was still finding all of this hard to believe, but she agreed to come out to take a picture with us. I encouraged Jesse, "You have the most beautiful baby girl, Jesse, and you have a great life ahead of you. Man, I'm telling you, God loves you, and that woman right there is going to make a great wife someday."

"That's right, man. She will."

We said goodbye and parted ways. Then a few weeks later they informed me that Jesse was doing really well.

Chapter 14

Raising the Standard

I believe the times are changing, and I believe the sons of this world are not going to be shrewder than the sons of the light, because God wants to use the church to reveal His manifold wisdom to the principalities.

> So the master commended the unjust steward because he had dealt shrewdly. For the sons of this world are more shrewd in their generation than the sons of light.
>
> –Luke 16:8

He wants to reveal the reality of His wisdom through His bride. And He wants the enemy to be afraid instead of the body of Christ being afraid. I am not going to water down the gospel to make you feel better about your succumbing to temptation. I'm going to speak the truth in love, I'm going to encourage you to stand fast in the midst of temptation, and I'm going to support you, but I will not pity you or help you make excuses. I will not keep you bound.

> No temptation has overtaken you except such as is common to man; but God is faithful, who will not allow you to be tempted beyond what you are able, but with the temptation will also make the way of escape, that you may be able to bear it.
>
> —1 Corinthians 10:13

It's unholy compassion to keep someone bound in pity. We are not to be in distress. Distress is for the devil. God is looking for champions, and when you said yes to Jesus, you became a champion. It's time that you wake up and see who you were created to be. Everywhere I go, I get to watch people burn for Jesus. Wouldn't you rather burn for the Lord instead of always being burned out? Grace is the fuel that enables you to keep burning.

> Go through, go through the gates! Prepare the way for the people; build up, build up the highway! Take out the stones, lift up a banner for the peoples!
>
> —Isaiah 62:10

"Prepare the way..." That sounds like a John the Baptist quote. Do you know that there are stumbling stones that we stumble over all the time? The stones on the path of the believer—the narrow path—need to be removed. The Lord told me He was raising me up to raise the standard in Christianity. He's raising the bar. He's putting it higher. It's not that I am higher, because I'm not. But if God can flow through me, He can flow through anybody. Dare to believe that God's Word is true!

What if we taught people from the start that they are brand-new creations? What if we taught people that the number one thing on God's priority list was renewing their minds? That's what I was taught from the very beginning.

"You're a brand-new creation."

"Yeah, but I don't feel like it."

"So what? You are!"

We don't walk by feelings; we walk by faith. And faith comes by the hearing of the Word of God.

> So then faith comes by hearing, and hearing by the word of God.
>
> —ROMANS 10:17

And we rely on the Holy Spirit to understand the Word. If we spend time alone in the secret place with Jesus, He said He would reward us in the open.

> But you, when you pray, go into your inner room, close your door and pray to your Father who is in secret, and your Father who sees what is done in secret will reward you.
>
> —MATTHEW 6:6, NASB

Knowing who we are in Jesus allows us to die to ourselves. Knowing who He is in us allows us to live for Him.

Dare to believe there is an open heaven wherever you go. We are all anointed men and women of God. This isn't just for the ministers on stage and the speakers on the front row of the church. Anyone can go out and share the gospel with people. When the kingdom of God possesses us, the truth overwhelms us so we must share the gospel. We must realize it is normal to share the gospel. It is normal to lay hands on the sick and see them recover. It is normal to have signs and wonders follow us because we are believers. God will show you things about people, and you'll know what to say because the Holy Spirit will give you the words they need to hear. You just start releasing what you have received. It's that simple.

I remember one time I was in Israel on a trip with Benny Hinn, about three years after I had received the baptism of the Holy Spirit and fire. I was thankful for all the Lord had done already, and I was pouring out everything I had received from the Lord to those around me, but I was still hungry for more of Him. One night, while we were in Israel, Benny was preaching. I knew I had to get down to the front, but I was in the back, and there were a lot of people. Miraculously I was able to get a seat up front, but by the time Benny had called for pastors and leaders to come stand up front for prayer and impartation, I was behind everyone again. I was so hungry for more of Jesus. I lifted my hands, and I felt electricity go down my arm, up to my chin, and across my face.

Suddenly Benny turned and yelled to the ushers, "Bring that man up here!"

The ushers came through the crowd, grabbed me, and brought me up on the stage. The presence of God was so strong, I couldn't stand up straight; the ushers were holding me up. Benny was way across from me on the stage. He prayed, "Jesus."

Right then a bolt of energy hit me and lifted both the ushers and me completely off the ground and threw us several yards backwards. Four times Benny prayed, and we went flying. Finally they laid my body down in front of the stage. The people I came with were able to find me because they had seen me on the cameras, flying across the stage. They transported me back to the hotel and put me in bed. From that point forward there was a noticeable increase of the manifested presence and power of the Holy Ghost on my life. When that happens, you get to represent Jesus in a way that people have never seen before. You have an amazing privilege to represent your King. You have this short window of opportunity called life, which is a gift from God. He's given it to you for you to live with a clean house, with a pure heart, and with clean hands. God wants to use you and flow through you. He wants to crush hell through you, but the first thing He wants to do is clean house.

The Word of God says to pursue peace and holiness, because without them no one will see the Lord.

> Pursue peace with all men, and the sanctification without which no one will see the Lord.
>
> —HEBREWS 12:14, NASB

We need to pursue peace. What does that mean? We need to pursue Jesus—He's the Prince of Peace. He is peace that surpasses understanding.

> And the peace of God, which surpasses all understanding, will guard your hearts and minds through Christ Jesus. Finally, brethren, whatever things are true, whatever things are noble, whatever things are just, whatever things are pure, whatever things are lovely, whatever things are of good report, if there is any virtue and if there is anything praiseworthy—meditate on these things.
>
> —Philippians 4:7–8

Jesus is saying that He has given you a peace that passes all understanding, which acts as a garrison to guard your heart and let you know what is right and what is wrong. Righteousness trains the senses to discern between good and evil. So when you are right with God, you have peace with God because you've been justified by faith. The peace you have with God is also a guard to discern whether something is OK. And then He tells you plainly what to set your mind upon: whatever things are true, etc. His peace actually builds a safeguard around your heart and mind in such a way that no lies can break through it undetected.

You need to understand the truth of who God says you are. It's about sonship and prioritizing relationship. God will help you see clearly. The Holy Spirit will reveal the Word to you to train you, admonish you, and build you up. The Word is used for rebuke, correction, and training your heart so that you will know the difference between good and evil–because righteousness trains the senses to discern between good and evil.

> All Scripture is given by inspiration of God, and is profitable for doctrine, for reproof, for correction, for instruction in righteousness, that the man of God may be complete, thoroughly equipped for every good work.
>
> –2 Timothy 3:16–17

You see, strong meat is for the mature, who have their senses trained to discern between good and evil. Ask God to convict you of the things that need to change and for the grace you need to obey when conviction comes, because delayed obedience is disobedience.

We can walk this way. We can live this way. We can burn this way so that people don't have to burn in hell one day.

There is a place in Christ we can live that is so powerful that there's no compromise at all inside of you. There's no need for attention or for the limelight. When you are the light, you don't need the limelight. Jesus didn't say, "This little light of mine, I'm going to let it shine." He said, "I am the light of the world!" Then He said, "You are the light of the world."

> Then Jesus spoke to them again, saying, "I am the light of the world. He who follows Me shall not walk in darkness, but have the light of life."
>
> –John 8:12

You are the light of the world. A city that is set on a hill cannot be hidden.

—MATTHEW 5:14

God saved me from myself and set me free from myself so that I could be free from you. No matter what you say to me, I can love you unconditionally—no strings attached. There's nothing you have to do to earn my love; I love you because I love God. But we only love God because He first loved us. We came to God because He first came to us. No matter how people come to Jesus, it's always the Father who called them in.

I study the Scriptures not to work myself into His approval but to show myself approved. I don't study the Word to preach a good sermon or to preach myself approved. I have already been approved by my Father, so I study to show myself approved so that my life is a reflection of what the Word says.

Be diligent to present yourself approved to God, a worker who does not need to be ashamed, rightly dividing the word of truth.

—2 TIMOTHY 2:15

Living a life that is a reflection of the Word is one of the most valuable things you can do. Keeping a pure conscience is vital because the more we sear our consciences, the more stuff that we allow, the more lines we cross, the more likely we are to begin to call good evil and call evil good.

...having faith and a good conscience, which some having rejected, concerning the faith have suffered shipwreck.

−1 TIMOTHY 1:19

Woe to those who call evil good, and good evil; who put darkness for light, and light for darkness; who put bitter for sweet, and sweet for bitter!

−ISAIAH 5:20

The Bible talks about this happening in the last days. There's a new grace doctrine going around out there, and it's from hell. I have a burning desire to dismantle that teaching. This doctrine makes people think grace is a license to do whatever you want. Grace is God's willingness to forgive me. Grace is God's willingness to empower me. Grace is God's willingness to come and make His home inside of me so that I can represent Him well. My using grace to sin would not be representing Him well. It would be representing hell, which isn't grace−it's disgrace.

I travel all over the world, and I get to see all these people. They say, "Hey, bro, you're all about grace, right?"

I say, "Yes, grace through faith."

See, legalism was taught for so long in the church that when the message of grace came, people took it to the other extreme of hyper grace. So the people who had been taught a doctrine of legalism all of their lives heard this distorted grace doctrine, and the pendulum swung the other way; they went into another error rather than into the truth. The hyper-grace message teaches that

God is OK with us staying in sin, because He understands that we are only human. That means people feel free to sin because God has already forgiven them; therefore they willfully continue to stay in their sin. That doctrine also teaches about one-time repentance, after which you can go on your way and eat, drink, and be merry. The hyper-grace doctrine is a reaction to error, and it is demonic. It's a defeat doctrine that leads to destruction. We cannot walk out the Word of God in our lives without the Holy Spirit. He's the One who wrote the Bible, so we can't do it without Him. We can't afford to be swayed by this twisted wind of doctrine. We have to be swayed by His love, by His heart, and by His beauty. We have to come back to His original plan, which is the desire of Jesus Christ.

Jesus has the sevenfold Spirit of God in Him, but His number one delight is the Spirit of the fear of the Lord.

> The Spirit of the LORD shall rest upon Him, the Spirit of wisdom and understanding, the Spirit of counsel and might, the Spirit of knowledge and of the fear of the LORD. His delight is in the fear of the LORD.
>
> —ISAIAH 11:2–3

The fear of the Lord is simply loving what God loves and despising what He despises. It's being so in reverential love with God that you wouldn't dare do evil now that you have Him. But it is through relationship that the fear of the Lord gets cultivated. God will point out things in your life that need to go, because He's the gardener; He clips, He prunes, and He trims.

He gets all this stuff out that needs to go, and then He expects obedience.

> I am the true vine, and My Father is the vinedresser. Every branch in Me that does not bear fruit, He takes away; and every branch that bears fruit, He prunes it so that it may bear more fruit. You are already clean because of the word which I have spoken to you. Abide in Me, and I in you. As the branch cannot bear fruit of itself unless it abides in the vine, so neither can you unless you abide in Me. I am the vine, you are the branches; he who abides in Me and I in him, he bears much fruit, for apart from Me you can do nothing. If anyone does not abide in Me, he is thrown away as a branch and dries up; and they gather them, and cast them into the fire and they are burned. If you abide in Me, and My words abide in you, ask whatever you wish, and it will be done for you. My Father is glorified by this, that you bear much fruit, and so prove to be My disciples. Just as the Father has loved Me, I have also loved you; abide in My love. If you keep My commandments, you will abide in My love; just as I have kept My Father's commandments and abide in His love. These things I have spoken to you so that My joy may be in you, and that your joy may be made full.
>
> —John 15:1–11, NASB

When God speaks to you with truth, grace empowers you to walk out whatever that truth calls you to. Without grace, truth is hard. But grace and truth came through Jesus.

Grace and truth came through Jesus Christ.

—John 1:17

We need both grace and truth. It's a combination. The Beatitudes say you are blessed when you're persecuted. That's truth, but grace also needs to come into play. Feeling blessed when you are persecuted may seem twisted, but by grace you can appreciate the value of suffering that has been granted to you when you are persecuted. The disciples were beaten and bleeding and counted it a privilege to suffer for their King.

Blessed are those who are persecuted for righteousness' sake, for theirs is the kingdom of heaven.

—Matthew 5:10

For to you it has been granted for Christ's sake, not only to believe in Him, but also to suffer for His sake, experiencing the same conflict which you saw in me, and now hear to be in me.

—Philippians 1:29–30, nasb

. . . that I may know Him and the power of His resurrection, and the fellowship of His sufferings, being conformed to His death, if, by any means, I may attain to the resurrection from the dead. Not that I have already attained, or am already perfected; but I press on, that I may lay hold of that for which Christ Jesus has also laid hold of me.

—Philippians 3:10–12

Yet we get uptight when we tell people Jesus loves them, and they snap at us because they don't want to hear it. There are those who say people get hurt by that because they have a spirit of rejection; they don't understand that the only one who has been rejected for eternity is the devil, and he wants himself in you. He tries to put his mindset in believers so they will think they have a spirit of rejection, but they don't. He can't come up to heaven and dethrone God. He tried that. It didn't work. God threw him out of there, and then He created us to triumph over the devil. I'm serious! God gets good pleasure out of watching His kids trample hell. He does! He loves it! It's so much more fun to stomp hell than it is to be manipulated by it. In order to not be manipulated by it, we have to understand who the Shepherd is, and we have to recognize the Shepherd's voice. God speaks through His Word.

Listen, you have to get the Word of God inside of you. If you go from Christian conference to conference to conference to get more of God, then you're deceived. Some Christians think, "I just need this man to lay hands on me. I just need another impartation!" I'm all for praying for people and laying hands on people. My question is: What are you doing with what you have already received from the Lord?

When I look at the life of Jesus, I see a life poured out in every way. Jesus was the Word of God made flesh, dwelling among men. We need to pour out what we have received from Him, just as He poured out what He received from the Father. You've got one life, one shot to give Jesus your all. According to the measure that you're willing to pour out your life into this gospel, according to the measure that you're willing to step out past yourself in an uncomfortable situation, and according to the measure that you're willing to give and lay your life down, God will pour back into you–good measure, pressed down, and running over. That's amazing!

> Give, and it will be given to you: good measure, pressed down, shaken together, and running over will be put into your bosom. For with the same measure that you use, it will be measured back to you.
>
> –LUKE 6:38

Some people try to tell Satan to "get behind them," and they spend their prayer time rebuking him. That's exactly what he wants! God never told us to do that. Why would I command Satan to get behind me when he already is? Jesus is the anchor of my soul.

> This hope we have as an anchor of the soul, both sure and steadfast, and which enters the Presence behind the veil.
>
> –HEBREWS 6:19

In the Bible, Peter explained that the prophets prophesied about a day when righteousness apart from the Law was coming. Jesus came to give us righteousness apart from walking out the Law. The salvation of our spirits happens when we are born again, but the salvation of our souls–the mind, will, and emotions–happens when we are transformed. God's grace is available to you both for salvation of your spirit and to reveal Christ to you in your soul. When Jesus is revealed to you in your soul, the enemy can no longer make you bankrupt in holiness, because your mind has been transformed by the revelation of Jesus and your oneness with Him. When the righteousness of Christ convicts your soul, the result is holiness and purity. When you have filled your mind up with God's thoughts, you're able to recognize twisted thoughts from the enemy and take those thoughts captive to the obedience of Christ.

> Though you have not seen Him, you love Him, and though you do not see Him now, but believe in Him, you greatly rejoice with joy inexpressible and full of glory, obtaining as the outcome of your faith the salvation of your souls.
>
> As to this salvation, the prophets who prophesied of the grace that would come to you made careful searches and inquiries, seeking to know what person or time the Spirit of Christ within them was indicating as He predicted the sufferings of Christ and the glories to follow. It was revealed to them that they were not serving themselves, but you, in these things which now have been announced to you through those who preached the gospel to you by the Holy Spirit sent from heaven—things into which angels long to look.
>
> Therefore, prepare your minds for action, keep sober in spirit, fix your hope completely on the grace to be brought to you at the revelation of Jesus Christ. As obedient children, do not be conformed to the former lusts which were yours in your ignorance, but like the

Holy One who called you, be holy yourselves also in all your behavior; because it is written, "You shall be holy, for I am holy."

—1 PETER 1:8–16, NASB

For the weapons of our warfare are not of the flesh, but divinely powerful for the destruction of fortresses. We are destroying speculations and every lofty thing raised up against the knowledge of God, and we are taking every thought captive to the obedience of Christ.

—2 CORINTHIANS 10:4–5, NASB

Now may the God of peace Himself sanctify you entirely; and may your spirit and soul and body be preserved complete, without blame at the coming of our Lord Jesus Christ.

—1 THESSALONIANS 5:23, NASB

The world is not looking for a confession from you. The world is looking for the real deal from you. A confession without a life lived by that confession is just empty words. It's just hot air. The Book of James says to receive with meekness the implanted Word, which can save your soul.

Therefore lay aside all filthiness and overflow of wickedness, and receive with meekness the implanted word, which is able to save your souls. But be doers of the word, and not hearers only, deceiving yourselves. For if anyone is a hearer of the word and not a doer, he is like a man observing his natural face in a mirror; for he observes himself, goes away, and immediately forgets what kind of man he was. But he who looks into the perfect law of liberty and continues in it, and is not a forgetful hearer but a doer of the work, this one will be blessed in what he does.

–JAMES 1:21–25

The Bible also says to not just be a hearer of the word but to be a doer. Don't just hear it; do it! How do you do it? You become it! Then all of a sudden the truth calls you to something, and you step into it and walk it out. We have complicated the simplicity of the gospel.

Oh, that you would bear with me in a little folly–and indeed you do bear with me. For I am jealous for you with godly jealousy. For I have betrothed you to one husband, that I may present you as a chaste virgin to Christ. But I fear, lest somehow, as the serpent deceived Eve by his craftiness, so your minds may be corrupted from the simplicity that is in Christ.

–2 CORINTHIANS 11:1–3

Jesus told us that we had to become like children or we would never enter His kingdom. We can't afford to think we have it all figured out. Being on fire for Jesus should not just be the visible excitement of the new believer in Christ; it should be a visible attribute of all believers, no matter how long they have been saved.

Truly I say to you, unless you are converted and become like children, you will not enter the kingdom of heaven.

—MATTHEW 18:3, NASB

Some people tell me that they have been Christians their whole lives and that I am lucky I came into Christianity the way I did, because they have a lot to unlearn. Our minds cannot unlearn; they must be renewed!

And do not be conformed to this world, but be transformed by the renewing of your mind, so that you may prove what the will of God is, that which is good and acceptable and perfect.

—ROMANS 12:2, NASB

God gave us minds to learn. It doesn't matter if you have been dead in the church for fifty years; the Holy Spirit can breathe on what you've learned and make it come to life! Outside of relationship with Jesus, you will memorize and memorize and beat yourself up, wondering why you can't walk out what truth calls you to. However, you can walk out the truth in a relationship with Jesus by spending time with Him alone in the secret place. Your mind becomes set on the things above, not beneath.

Set your mind on things above, not on things on the earth.

—COLOSSIANS 3:2

For where your treasure is, there your heart will be
also.

—Matthew 6:21

God gives us His thoughts, which are higher than our
thoughts, and He shows us His ways, which are higher
than our ways. And the more we commune with Him, the
more we become like Him.

> For as the heavens are higher than the earth, so are
> My ways higher than your ways, and My thoughts than
> your thoughts.
>
> —Isaiah 55:9

You cannot continue to spend time with Jesus and
remain bound in your sins. You see, we have been given
the mind of Christ.

> And I, brethren, when I came to you, did not come
> with excellence of speech or of wisdom declaring to
> you the testimony of God. For I determined not to
> know anything among you except Jesus Christ and
> Him crucified. I was with you in weakness, in fear, and
> in much trembling. And my speech and my preaching
> were not with persuasive words of human wisdom, but
> in demonstration of the Spirit and of power, that your
> faith should not be in the wisdom of men but in the
> power of God.
>
> However, we speak wisdom among those who are
> mature, yet not the wisdom of this age, nor of the rulers
> of this age, who are coming to nothing. But we speak the

wisdom of God in a mystery, the hidden wisdom which God ordained before the ages for our glory, which none of the rulers of this age knew; for had they known, they would not have crucified the Lord of glory.

But as it is written: "Eye has not seen, nor ear heard, nor have entered into the heart of man the things which God has prepared for those who love Him." But God has revealed them to us through His Spirit. For the Spirit searches all things, yes, the deep things of God. For what man knows the things of a man except the spirit of the man which is in him? Even so no one knows the things of God except the Spirit of God. Now we have received, not the spirit of the world, but the Spirit who is from God, that we might know the things that have been freely given to us by God.

These things we also speak, not in words which man's wisdom teaches but which the Holy Spirit teaches, comparing spiritual things with spiritual. But the natural man does not receive the things of the Spirit of God, for they are foolishness to him; nor can he know them, because they are spiritually discerned. But he who is spiritual judges all things, yet he himself is rightly judged by no one. For "who has known the mind of the LORD that he may instruct Him?" But we have the mind of Christ.

—1 CORINTHIANS 2:1–16

When we get to know Jesus and the way He thinks, everything changes. If you want to break bad habits, make spending time with Jesus your habit. As you focus on Him and see the reality of sonship, all of a sudden the things that used to compete for your attention fade away.

Worship Jesus in the secret place. When you seek Jesus in the secret place, He rewards you in the open place. Seek Him in order to know Him. We have to know Him. We have to realize what He has done for us. You know, all of us have equally sinned and He has equally forgiven us. Some people compare themselves to others and say, "They did worse than me, then they were touched by Jesus, and that's why they love so much." But statements such as that are wrong because sin is sin, and all of us have sinned and fallen short of God's glory.

> For all have sinned and fall short of the glory of God.
> —ROMANS 3:23

When we see that we have sinned before God and that He has cleansed us from all unrighteousness, our consciences are cleansed, and we won't want to violate our consciences ever again.[1]

> But the goal of our instruction is love from a pure heart and a good conscience and a sincere faith.
> —1 TIMOTHY 1:5, NASB

The result is that we will live our lives on fire, shining as a light to a wicked and perverse generation.

> ...that you may become blameless and harmless, children of God without fault in the midst of a crooked

and perverse generation, among whom you shine as
lights in the world.

—PHILIPPIANS 2:15

We have all been called to the same thing: to
walk like Jesus!

Therefore be imitators of God, as beloved children.

—EPHESIANS 5:1, NASB

You were darkness, but now you are light! I was
twisted, but God transferred me into the light of His Son
through the gospel.

For He rescued us from the domain of darkness, and
transferred us to the kingdom of His beloved Son.

—COLOSSIANS 1:13, NASB

The Bible says, "You are the light of the world."

You are the light of the world. A city set on a hill cannot be hidden.

—MATTHEW 5:14, NASB

The places of the world are dark until you show up.
The moment you arrive, the light has come. That's not
arrogance; that's confidence in who God has called you
to be. For example, if you go to a place where there are
a bunch of witches, the moment you show up, the light
shows up, and the darkness they carry no longer matters.
Heaven is going to come because you did. When you're

in love with Jesus and your confidence comes from the reality of righteousness, then you are as bold as a lion. The righteous do not shrink back!

> The wicked flee when no one is pursuing, but the righteous are bold as a lion.
>
> —PROVERBS 28:1, NASB

Love doesn't hide. Love has no fear. Love is as bold as a lion. We are to go into all the world as a living, breathing, walking, talking fireball of light.

> There is no fear in love; but perfect love casts out fear, because fear involves torment. But he who fears has not been made perfect in love.
>
> —1 JOHN 4:18

It's time to burn with a fire. It's time to blaze. It's time to light up your workplace. It's time to not be ashamed of the gospel. The worst thing you can do is be silent. It's time to be bold about what you say you believe. You need to be unashamed of the gospel, for it is the power of God unto salvation for them that believe.

> For I am not ashamed of the gospel of Christ, for it is the power of God to salvation for everyone who believes, for the Jew first and also for the Greek.
>
> —ROMANS 1:16

The word *believe* means to be fully convinced, without a shadow of a doubt. Are you fully convinced beyond a shadow of a doubt that you're going to heaven? If your answer is yes, great! That's the end result of a life fully lived. Now let me ask you this: Are you fully convinced that heaven got into you? This is what I'm talking about. You can position yourself to get out of here and go to heaven, but Jesus told us to be of good cheer because He overcame the world, which means you can overcome too! Make Jesus your everything. You don't know how long you have on this planet to make an impact for the kingdom of God. Life is short—leave a legacy!

> These things I have spoken to you, so that in Me you may have peace. In the world you have tribulation, but take courage; I have overcome the world.
>
> —JOHN 16:33, NASB

He overcame the world, so why would we feel threatened by it? We must not be afraid. We must not be threatened. We must be set aflame for Jesus. We must be a people so possessed by God that everywhere we go—in every city, every town, every tribe, every nation, every place on the earth where there is a Christian—people just see Him.

My final question to you is this: What are you going to do with what the Lord has given you?

References

Chapter 1

1. *Merriam-Webster*, s.v. "testimony," accessed April 16, 2020, https://www.merriam-webster.com/dictionary/testimony.
2. Blue Letter Bible, s.v. "*martyria*," accessed April 16, 2020, https://www.blueletterbible.org/lang/lexicon/lexicon.cfm?Strongs=G3141&t=KJV.

Chapter 7

1. "LifeWay Research: Americans Are Fond of the Bible, Don't Actually Read It," LifeWay, April 25, 2017, https://lifewayresearch.com/2017/04/25/lifeway-research-americans-are-fond-of-the-bible-dont-actually-read-it/.

Chapter 14

1. See the following Scriptures on having a cleansed conscience: Acts 23:1; 24:16; 2 Corinthians 1:12; 1 Timothy 1:19; 3:9; 2 Timothy 1:3; Titus 1:15; Hebrews 9:14; 10:22.